Elizabeth I and Foreign
Policy, 1558–1603

IN THE SAME SERIES

General Editors: Eric J. Evans and P.D. King

Lynn Abrams	Bismarck and the German Empire 1871–1918
David Arnold	The Age of Discovery 1400–1600
A.L. Beier	The Problem of the Poor in Tudor and Early Stuart England
Martin Blinkhorn	Democracy and Civil War in Spain 1931–1939
Martin Blinkhorn	Mussolini and Fascist Italy
Robert M. Bliss	Restoration England 1660–1688
Stephen Constantine	Lloyd George
Stephen Constantine	Social Conditions in Britain 1918–1939
Susan Doran	Elizabeth I and Religion 1558–1603
Christopher Durston	Charles I
Christopher Durston	James I
Eric J. Evans	The Great Reform Act of 1832
Eric J. Evans	Political Parties in Britain 1783–1867
Eric J. Evans	Sir Robert Peel
Eric J. Evans	William Pitt the Younger
T.G. Fraser	Ireland in Conflict, 1922–1998
Peter Gaunt	The British Wars 1637–1651
Dick Geary	Hitler and Nazism
John Gooch	The Unification of Italy
Alexander Grant	Henry VII
M.J. Heale	The American Revolution
M.J. Heale	Franklin D. Roosevelt
Ruth Henig	The Origins of the First World War
Ruth Henig	The Origins of the Second World War 1933–1939
Ruth Henig	Versailles and After 1919–1933
Ruth Henig	The Weimar Republic 1919–1933
P.D. King	Charlemagne
Stephen J. Lee	Peter the Great

Stephen J. Lee	The Thirty Years War
John Lowe	Britain and Foreign Affairs 1815–1885
J.M. MacKenzie	The Partition of Africa 1880–1900
John W. Mason	The Cold War 1945–1991
Michael Mullett	Calvin
Michael Mullett	The Counter-Reformation
Michael Mullett	James II and English Politics 1678–1688
Michael Mullett	Luther
D.G. Newcombe	Henry VIII and the English Reformation
Robert Pearce	Attlee's Labour Governments 1945–1951
Gordon Phillips	The Rise of the Labour Party 1893–1931
John Plowright	Regency England
Hans A. Pohlsander	The Emperor Constantine
Roger Price	Napoleon III and the Second Empire
J.H. Shennan	France before the Revolution
J.H. Shennan	International Relations in Europe 1689–1789
J.H. Shennan	Louis XIV
Margaret Shennan	The Rise of Brandenburg-Prussia
David Shotter	Augustus Caesar
David Shotter	The Fall of the Roman Republic
David Shotter	Nero
David Shotter	Tiberius Caesar
Richard Stoneman	Alexander the Great
Keith J. Stringer	The Reign of Stephen
John Thorley	Athenian Democracy
Geoffrey Treasure	Richelieu and Mazarin
John K. Walton	Chartism
John K. Walton	Disraeli
John K. Walton	The Second Reform Act
Michael J. Winstanley	Gladstone and the Liberal Party
Michael J. Winstanley	Ireland and the Land Question 1800–1922
Alan Wood	The Origins of the Russian Revolution 1861–1917
Alan Wood	Stalin and Stalinism
Austin Woolrych	England Without a King 1649–1660

LANCASTER PAMPHLETS

Elizabeth I and Foreign Policy, 1558–1603

Susan Doran

London and New York

First published 2000
by Routledge
11 New Fetter Lane, London EC4P 4EE

Simultaneously published in the USA and Canada
by Routledge
29 West 35th Street, New York, NY 10001

Routledge is an imprint of the Taylor & Francis Group

Typeset in Bembo by Taylor & Francis Ltd
Printed and bound in Great Britain by MPG Books Ltd, Bodmin

British Library Cataloguing in Publication Data
A catalogue record for this book is available from the British Library

Library of Congress Cataloging in Publication Data
Doran, Susan.
Elizabeth I and foreign relations / Susan Doran.
p. cm.
Includes bibliographical references (p.).
1. Great Britain–Foreign policy–1558–1603. 2. Elizabeth I, Queen of
England, 1533–1603–Views on foreign relations. I. Title: Elizabeth the
First and foreign policy.
II. Title
DA356 D678 2000
942.05'092–dc21   99–048895

ISBN 0–415–15355–7

TO MY PARENTS

CONTENTS

Maps   x
Genealogical charts   xiii
Chronology   xvi
Glossary   xix

1 Background: English Foreign Policy before 1558   1

2 New Problems 1558–68   6

3 Traditional Directions in Foreign Policy 1558–68   13
The Habsburg Alliance   13
Scotland   16
France   21

4 Crisis Management 1568–85   25
1568–73   27
1574–81   34
1581–85   41

5 The Contemporary Debate over Policy 1558–85   45

6 War 1585–1603   51

7 Conclusions   63

Select Bibliography   71

Map 1 The Netherlands (areas which returned to Spanish control 1581–8 are hatched)

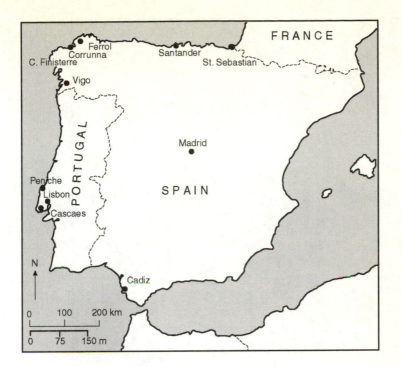

Map 2 Spain and Portugal

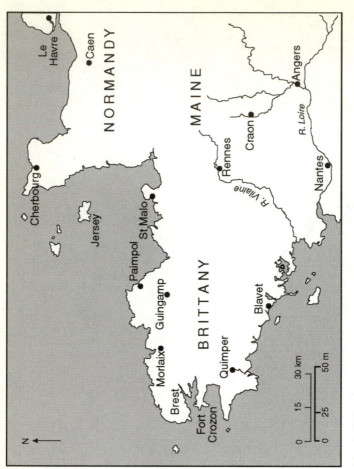

Map 3 Brittany

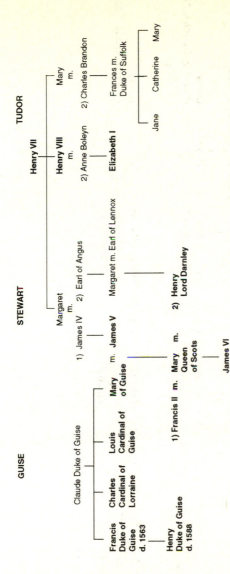

GUISE

Claude Duke of Guise

Charles Cardinal of Lorraine

Louis Cardinal of Guise

Mary of Guise

Francis Duke of Guise d. 1563

Henry Duke of Guise d. 1588

1) **Francis II**

STEWART

Margaret m.

1) James IV   2) Earl of Angus

James V   m.

Margaret m. Earl of Lennox

m. **Mary Queen of Scots**

2) **Henry Lord Darnley**

James VI

TUDOR

Henry VII

Henry VIII m.

2) Anne Boleyn

Elizabeth I

Mary m.

2) Charles Brandon

Frances m. Duke of Suffolk

Jane   Catherine   Mary

Figures in bold are those who appear in main part of the text

Chart 1   Mary Queen of Scots and the Guise Family

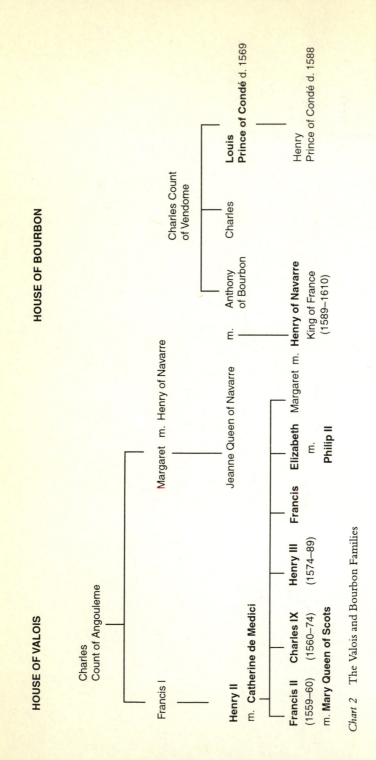

Chart 2   The Valois and Bourbon Families

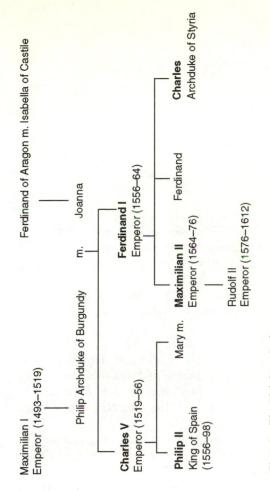

Maximilian I
Emperor (1493–1519)

Ferdinand of Aragon m. Isabella of Castile

Philip Archduke of Burgundy

Joanna

m.

Charles V
Emperor (1519–56)

Ferdinand I
Emperor (1556–64)

Philip II
King of Spain
(1556–98)

Mary m.

Maximilian II
Emperor (1564–76)

Ferdinand

Charles
Archduke of Styria

Rudolf II
Emperor (1576–1612)

Chart 3   The Habsburg Rulers

CHRONOLOGY

1558	Loss of Calais (Jan.). Mary Queen of Scots married dauphin (Apr.). Accession of Elizabeth I (Nov.).
1559	Peace of Cateau-Cambresis (3 Apr.). Protestant rebellion in Scotland (May). Accession of Francis II (July).
1560	Treaty of Berwick (Feb.). Assault on Leith. Treaty of Edinburgh (July). Accession of Charles IX (Dec.).
1561	Mary's return to Scotland (Aug.).
1562	Final session of Council of Trent. First Civil War in France (Mar.). Treaty of Hampton Court with Huguenots (Sep.). English occupation of Le Havre.
1563	Surrender of Le Havre (July). Embargo on English trade to Netherlands (Nov.).
1564	Resumption of Habsburg marriage-negotiations.
1565	Bayonne interview (June). Mary's marriage to Lord Darnley (July).
1566	Political and religious unrest in Netherlands (summer).
1567	Mary's deposition (July). Alva's arrival in Netherlands (Aug.). End of Habsburg matrimonial negotiations (Dec.).
1568	Mary's flight to England (May). San Juan de Ulúa (Sep.). Affair of Genoese treasure (Dec.).
1569	Suspension of Anglo-Spanish trade (Jan.). Northern Rising (Oct.).
1570	Assassination of Regent Moray in Scotland (Jan.). Papal bull of excommunication (Feb.).

1571	Anglo–French matrimonial negotiations. Discovery of Ridolfi plot. Civil War in Scotland.
1572	Treaty of Blois (Apr.). Sea Beggars' capture of Brill (Apr.). Massacre of St Bartholomew (Aug.).
1573	Siege of La Rochelle. Resumption of Anglo-Spanish trade (Mar.).
1574	Accession of Henry III (May).
1576	Peace of Monsieur in France (May). 'Spanish Fury' at Antwerp (4–7 Nov.). Pacification of Ghent (8 Nov.).
1577	Perpetual Edict (Feb.). Start of Drake's voyage of 'circumnavigation' (Nov.).
1578	Battle of Gembloux (Jan.). Anjou matrimonial negotiations.
1579	Reconciliation of southern Netherlands' provinces with Philip II (May). Papal-backed expedition to Ireland (July). D'Aubigny's arrival in Scotland (Sep.).
1580	Execution of Regent Morton in Scotland. Philip II's invasion of Portugal (Aug.). Massacre of Smerwick (Nov.).
1581	Drake knighted by queen (Apr.).
1582	Anjou's expedition to Netherlands (Feb.). Parma's victories in Flanders and Brabant.
1584	Expulsion of De Mendoza (Jan.). Death of Anjou (June). Assassination of William of Orange (July). Treaty of Joinville (Dec.).
1585	Treaty of Nonsuch (Aug.). Drake's expedition to Galicia and Caribbean (Sep.). Leicester's arrival in Netherlands (Dec.).
1586	Treaty of Berwick with James VI (July). Battle of Zutphen (Sep.).
1587	Betrayal of Deventer (Jan.). Drake's raid on Cadiz (Apr.).
1588	Defeat of Spanish Armada (Aug.).
1589	Portugal expedition (Apr.). Assassination of Henry III and accession of Henry IV (July). Willoughby's expedition to Normandy (Sep.).
1590	Parma's invasion of France (July). Spanish landing in Brittany (Oct.).
1591	Norris' expedition to Brittany (May). Siege of Rouen (Oct.).

1593	Henry IV's conversion to Catholicism (July).
1594	Henry IV's occupation of Paris (Mar.). Fall of Groningen (June). Brest campaign (Sep.). Capture of Crozon (Nov.).
1595	Tyrone rebellion (May). Panama expedition.
1596	Cadiz expedition.
1597	Azores expedition.
1598	Treaty of Vervins (May). Accession of Philip III of Spain (Sep.).
1601	Spanish landing at Kinsale (Sep.).
1602	Surrender of Spanish in Ireland (Jan.).
1603	Death of Elizabeth (Mar.).

GLOSSARY

Terms used are marked ★ in the text.

Anglophile   a supporter of England.

Burgundy   the lands ruled by the duke of Burgundy. These included the seventeen provinces of the Netherlands. At the beginning of Elizabeth's reign Philip II ruled these territories.

Catholic League   local leagues set up in France in 1576 with the aim of defending the Catholic faith. A new league was formed in 1584 with Henry Duke of Guise at its head.

Cautionary towns   the towns delivered to Elizabeth in the Netherlands as sureties for her loans and military help.

Dauphin   French king's first born son.

Dynastic   connected to a family of hereditary rulers.

Hanse   a league of North German and Baltic trading towns.

Harquebus   portable firearm.

Heir presumptive   the person who was next in line to the throne but not the eldest son of the monarch. If the monarch died immediately, the heir presumptive would take the throne but his/her right might be removed by the birth of a nearer heir.

Huguenots   French Calvinists.

Iberian   Spanish and Portuguese.

Inquisition   an institution with special jurisdiction to deal with heresy.

Lutheran princes   those rulers who had adopted the Protestant religion as formulated by Martin Luther. In Germany these included the dukes of Saxony, Hesse and Brandenburg. The kings of Sweden and Denmark were also Lutherans in this period.

Merchant Adventurers   the company of London merchants who had a monopoly of trade in cloth to the Netherlands.

Portugal   when the king of Portugal died in 1579 a dispute arose over the succession. Philip II was one of the claimants and used his army in 1580 to win the throne. Elizabeth backed Dom Antonio, another of the pretenders.

Privateers   sea captains who held authorisation to attack enemy shipping. Those who plundered ships without such a commission were pirates.

Sea Beggars   the name given to the Calvinist exiles from the Netherlands who continued the struggle against the duke of Alva. They frequently acted as privateers.

Staple   a town appointed by royal authority in which a group of merchants had exclusive rights of purchase over certain classes of goods to be exported.

States   the body representing the different provinces of the Netherlands. After 1576 it became the central organ of government which negotiated with foreign powers.

Union of Arras   a union of the provinces of Hainaut, Artois and Walloon Flanders. It was formed in January 1579 with the intention of making peace with Spain.

Union of Utrecht   a union of the provinces Holland, Zealand, Utrecht, Friesland, Gelderland and the Ommelanden formed in January 1579 to continue the war against Spain.

1

BACKGROUND

English Foreign Policy before 1558

For most of the late medieval and early Tudor period, English foreign policy rested upon twin pillars: hostility towards the kings of France and friendship with the rulers of Burgundy*. Conflict with the former arose from competing dynastic* claims to lands and titles in France as well as rivalry over influence in Scotland. Amity with the duke of Burgundy, who ruled the Netherlands, was based on mutual economic interests and a shared hostility towards France.

Anglo-French conflict originated in the Norman period, when the English dukes of Normandy vied for power with their neighbour and overlord, the king of France. It entered a new phase, however, when Edward III laid claim to the French throne in 1337, and at the same time attempted to win back the ancestral lands of Normandy, Anjou, Poitou and Gascony which had been lost during the previous century. Thanks largely to the skill of the English longbowmen, Edward III enjoyed notable victories at Crécy (1346) and Poitiers (1356), and the French king was forced to recognise his title to the duchy of Aquitaine. Henry V, who resumed the war soon after his accession in 1413, won the still more famous battle of Agincourt in 1415, conquered much of Normandy, and was recognised as the heir of the French dauphin. During his son's reign (Henry VI 1422–61, 1470–1), however, English successes were reversed. Civil strife within England coincided with the political recovery of the French monarch, and undermined the English military effort. Furthermore, the French started to use artillery, which gave them the advantage in battle. As a result, England lost Normandy in 1450 and Gascony in 1453; all that remained of its French empire was the pale of Calais.

Brought up on heroic tales of chivalry, Henry VIII's dream was to emulate Henry V by winning honour in battle, regaining the lost lands in France and making good his claim to the French crown. But, after some initial successes, Henry found that he lacked the financial resources to keep his army in the field during the early 1520s. The result was that he was unable to benefit from the overwhelming victory of his ally, the Holy Roman Emperor Charles V, against Francis I of France at the battle of Pavia (1525). It was only after his revenues had been boosted by the spoils of ecclesiastical property that Henry could again attempt to win glory and territory in France, but this time he contented himself with the capture of some towns in Picardy near Calais. In 1544 his army captured Boulogne, but two years later he agreed to the Treaty of the Campe which made provision for the French king to purchase the town after eight years. The cost of the war against France and the garrisoning of Boulogne had proved too high to continue indefinitely, and Henry was forced to accept that military adventures on the continent were out of the question for the time being.

During the early years of the next reign, it became even more apparent that war against France, whether on the Continent or in Scotland, was beyond the means of the English king. For this reason, the Edwardian privy council signed a peace-treaty with Henry II of France in 1550, which handed over Boulogne some years early. Similarly, Mary I (1553–58) wanted peace with France, despite her marriage to Charles V's son, Philip of Spain. Had Henry II not acted in an aggressive way towards England, she might well have avoided being drawn into her husband's war against the French. As it was, English troops joined with Philip II's army to win a victory at the battle of St Quentin. Soon afterwards, however, the French invaded the English pale and captured Calais in January 1558; it was the most humiliating defeat for England in the Tudor period (Doran 1999).

In addition to disputes over titles and lands in France, the French and English monarchs competed for influence in Scotland. The problem here was also long standing. Since the reign of Edward I, English kings had claimed lordship over their Scottish counterpart and asserted that he owed them homage. In response to these theoretical claims and to Edward I's invasions, the Scots turned to France for protection and in 1295 signed an alliance with Philip IV. Thereafter, the alliance (to be known as the 'Auld Alliance') was renewed whenever the Scots felt threatened by the English monarch or their king wanted to assert independence of action. During Henry VIII's reign, the 'Auld Alliance' was responsible for the outbreak of a war in 1513 and again in 1542. On the former occasion, James IV of Scotland invaded northern England to assist his ally Louis XII after Henry had set out with his troops to fight against France. James' defeat and death at the battle of Flodden (1513) temporarily ended the danger from Scotland. In the mid 1530s, however, his son (James V), who had by then reached adulthood, began rebuilding the French connection. Unable to rely on James V's loyalty, Henry decided to bolt his back door before embarking on his new project of war in France. Thus, in 1542 he ordered his army to attack the Scots, who suffered a major defeat at the battle of Solway Moss. With the death of James three weeks later, Henry saw an opportunity for controlling Scotland by arranging a dynastic marriage between his own son Prince Edward and James' baby daughter Mary Queen of Scots. Perceiving a threat to their national independence, the Scots resisted. The subsequent 'Rough Wooing' of Queen Mary resulted in six years of Anglo-Scottish warfare (1544–50).

On Henry VIII's death in January 1546, Lord Protector Somerset made the Scottish War the priority of his government's policy, and an army entered Scotland to crush opposition to the marriage. The aim was to establish a union of the two realms and to extend the Protestant Reformation into Scotland. But, despite an initial victory in pitched battle at Pinkie (1547), the policy was a dismal failure. Somerset's strategy of establishing garrisons in the Lowlands, which were designed to control the surrounding areas, alienated the Scots, even those who were his political allies, and proved horrendously expensive to maintain. Henry II of France, moreover, could not afford to allow his ally to be swallowed up by his enemy, and consequently sent some 10,000 men to Scotland. Mary was carried off to France, while the French troops joined in the Scottish attacks on the English garrisons. As a result of this intervention, England was forced to evacuate Scotland. By the end of Edward VI's reign, therefore, the northern kingdom was little more than a French satellite. Its monarch was residing in France and betrothed to the dauphin; and after 1554 its regent was the French-born Mary of Guise, the widow of James V, who ruled with the help of French bureaucrats.

It was chiefly the need for allies against France that caused English monarchs to develop a close relationship with the dukes of Burgundy. In the early fifteenth century (especially the years 1419–35) the dukes acted as active allies against the kings of France, who were their feudal overlord and political rival. At the end of the century, the dukes had become Habsburg princes: first Philip (1482–1506), the son of Emperor Maximilian I, and then Charles (1506–56), who became king of Spain in 1516 and was elected Emperor Charles V in 1519. The Habsburgs were rivals of the French king in other areas of Europe, particularly Italy and Navarre, and were at war against the kings of France at regular intervals from 1512 until 1559. Henry VIII, consequently, had little difficulty in negotiating a Habsburg alliance against Louis XII in 1512 or against Francis I in 1521 and 1543. The Habsburgs, however, were unreliable partners, who frequently failed to give Henry much-needed military backing and signed separate (if temporary) treaties of peace with France whenever it suited them. The 'ancient amity' with the Burgundian rulers, therefore, was not without its strains.

A new dimension to Anglo-Habsburg tensions arose, however, when Henry discarded his wife, Catherine of Aragon, the aunt of Charles V, and broke with the papacy. On several occasions in the late 1530s, Charles threatened a crusade against England, leading Henry VIII to consider forming an alliance with the Lutheran princes★ of Germany, who had also broken with the pope and established Protestant churches in their own territories. In addition, until her accession as queen, Charles posed as the protector of Catherine's daughter Mary, who increasingly came under pressure to change her religious allegiance and practices. Although the emperor actually did very little to aid Mary, she looked to him for guidance, and soon after her accession she married his son, Philip, against the wishes of many in her court and council. This Habsburg marriage alliance eventually brought England into war against France (April 1557), a war which became increasingly unpopular after the capture of Calais in January 1558, especially as the economic burdens in England were growing unacceptably heavy.

In the early Tudor period, shared economic interests helped the maintenance of close ties between the rulers of England and Burgundy, and proved instrumental in preventing political difficulties between them from escalating into open warfare. In the fifteenth century, Antwerp in the Netherlands had become the destination for English woollen cloth exports and the centre of financial services used by merchants and monarch alike. This traffic was immensely profitable both for the Merchant Adventurers★ and for English monarchs, who raked in the dues from customs. England's merchants, moreover, enjoyed substantial commercial privileges in the Netherlands by dint of the commercial treaty

4

known as the *Magnus Intercursus* (1496). The advantages were not just one-way however; the Netherlands also gained from this commercial relationship. The import of unfinished English cloth stimulated textile manufacturing in the finishing processes and attracted international traders to Antwerp. As a result Antwerp became a boom city, doubling its population in the first half of the sixteenth century (Ramsey 1975). Any disturbance to its trade with England could destabilise its economy and create political difficulties for its ruler.

To sum up, Elizabeth I inherited a strong commercial relationship with the Netherlands, a tradition of friendship with its rulers and a long history of wars against France and Scotland. In recent years, however, this warfare had failed to bring any political advantages to England. The English army had defeated the French and Scots in battle, but the victories had not been followed up by political successes. Henry VIII had won Boulogne, but it had brought him no nearer to the French crown and had proved an expensive outpost which could not be retained. Mary's troops had helped Philip win a useful victory, but her garrisons in the Calais pale had been unable to ward off a French assault. England had won three pitched battles in Scotland between 1513 and 1547, but its political leaders could not bring an end to the 'Auld Alliance' nor secure control over its northern neighbour by force, persuasion or dynastic union. Foreign policy in the first part of the sixteenth century had therefore been for the most part assertive, even aggressive, but generally ineffectual. The wars, furthermore, had proved so difficult to finance that they had drained the crown's resources and imposed an onerous burden on the economy. Between 1538 and 1552, the English crown spent about £3.5 million on wars against France and Scotland, a sum raised by loans, the debasement of the currency, and the sale of crown lands. In 1558 Elizabeth inherited a debt of £300,000, which was only paid off in 1578. At Elizabeth's accession in November 1558, therefore, many members of the political elite were disillusioned by continental warfare and demoralised by the military and political defeats against France and Scotland.

2

NEW PROBLEMS 1558–68

Elizabeth I came to power just when the military, political and religious maps of Europe were beginning to change. During the first half of the century, France and the Habsburg Empire were the two major military powers in Europe, with England a respected second-runner. Thus, Francis I and Henry II of France proved capable of putting large armies into the field to challenge the might of Charles V, while Henry VIII was a much sought-after ally. During the second half of the sixteenth century, however, Spain came to be the pre-eminent power in Europe. In 1567, its army stationed in the Netherlands comprised 10,000 men; soon afterwards it was augmented to 50,000; and at its peak of strength in 1574 the governor-general in the Netherlands formed an army of some 86,000 men. Philip II's naval force was also impressive: Spanish galleons contributed to the Holy League's victory over the Turks at Lepanto (1571); and the armadas against England were formidable both in the number and size of their ships. The French monarchs, on the other hand, were militarily and financially weakened by a series of civil wars, which ran from 1563 to 1598. France consequently could provide no effective counterbalance to Spain. Indeed, in the early Elizabethan period, only the Turks provided a military challenge to the Spanish Empire, and distracted Philip II from asserting his power in northern Europe. After 1577, however, the Turks signed a series of truces with Spain, thereby freeing the king to pursue expansionist policies.

As far as England's military power was concerned, Elizabeth could barely compete with the French kings, never mind Philip II. Since England's population was significantly lower than that of both France and Spain, fewer men were eligible for conscription. Warfare, moreover, was becoming more expensive and Elizabeth could not afford to put large numbers of troops in the field even for relatively short campaigns; a standing army was simply out of the question. The English army was way behind its European rivals in technology and training. It lacked sufficient artillery to take Leith from the French in 1560, and in 1588 was still making use of the longbow, which was by then an outmoded form of armament on the Continent. Regular training of troops only began in England after 1572, whereas it was usual in mid-century Europe. A new logistical difficulty was introduced with the loss of Calais; without a bridgehead on the Continent, military adventures abroad were impossible unless allies provided an operational base. In these circumstances, Elizabeth had to think very carefully before raising an army to fight in overseas campaigns.

The most striking political development in Europe evident at Elizabeth's accession was the dismantling of Charles V's vast empire. In 1555 Charles V had been forced to concede a degree of religious toleration to the Lutheran princes* in Germany. Disillusioned and exhausted by his failure to preserve the unity of Christendom, Charles abdicated and divided his inheritance. He handed over Habsburg territories in Italy, the Americas, the Netherlands, Franche-Comté and Spain to his son Philip, and bequeathed his Austrian lands and imperial title to his brother Ferdinand. As a result of this partition, the Netherlands were no longer the geographical centre of Charles V's *monarchia*, but instead an offshoot of the Spanish empire. The departure of Philip II in August 1559 from the Netherlands to Spain symbolised its change in status; but it also had practical repercussions that created problems in Anglo–Spanish relations. Philip never again visited the Netherlands and thus had no opportunity for arranging personal meetings with Elizabeth, which might have been useful for dissolving suspicions and smoothing over difficulties between the two rulers. In the absence of such interviews, both monarchs became entirely dependent on the skill and goodwill of their resident ambassadors for building up trust and resolving disputes between them. Unfortunately their representatives were rarely up to the job. As far as Elizabeth's resident ambassadors to Spain were concerned, Sir Thomas Chalonner proved a competent diplomat in his embassy of 1561 to 1565, but his successor John Man

(1566–68) lacked the necessary tact to carry out his mission successfully and was expelled in the spring of 1568. He had particularly offended Philip by referring to the pope disparagingly and openly praising the Huguenot★ rebels. His demands for personal freedom of worship also went down badly at the Spanish court. Since he was never replaced, there was no one to represent Elizabeth's interests or present the English point of view at Madrid. Nor was Elizabeth well informed about Spanish policy. As for Philip II's ambassadors to England, only Guzman de Silva (1564–68) proved sympathetic and adept at developing good relations with the queen and her leading ministers. The remainder ended their period of office in disgrace because of their involvement in Catholic intrigues. Perhaps the most disastrous was Guerau de Spes (1568–72), though Bernardino de Mendoza (1578–84) ran him a close second. These two did considerable damage to Anglo–Spanish relations: they fostered the belief in England that Philip II and his agents were plotting to overthrow Elizabeth, and helped to convince Philip that Elizabeth was at the centre of an international Protestant conspiracy to incite rebellion in the Netherlands and France. De Spes' incompetence was largely responsible for the rupture in Anglo–Spanish relations in January 1569 (Ramsey 1984).

An even more important change in international politics concerned religion. During the first half of the sixteenth century, international relations were essentially dynastic★ in character, notwithstanding Martin Luther's break with Rome in 1521 which came to divide Lutherans from Catholics. Until 1559 the rivalry between the Habsburgs and the kings of France eclipsed confessional conflicts. Indeed the Habsburg–Valois Wars so dominated international affairs that the Catholic Charles V tried to form an alliance with Henry VIII, after his own break with the papacy, rather than unite with Francis I in a crusade against him. Similarly, despite their own religious orthodoxy, both Francis I and Henry II of France gave aid to the Lutheran princes of Germany against Charles V. At the same time, English rulers felt little solidarity with European Protestants. Henry VIII refused to sign up to the 1530 Augsburg Confession of Faith of the German Lutherans and join the Schmalkadic League of Lutheran towns and princes. Edward VI's ministers also remained aloof from the League and stayed neutral when the Lutheran princes took up arms against the emperor in 1547 and 1551. All this changed, however, during Elizabeth's reign. In the 1560s there seemed to be a hardening of the confessional divide in Europe.

8

After 1555, the confessional conflict between the German Lutheran princes and the emperor subsided. In that year, the peace of Augsburg was signed, which gave the German Lutheran princes the right to follow their own religion and cleared the way for their peaceful co-existence with the emperor and other Catholic rulers. A new source of religious conflict within Europe, however, soon arose with the spread of Calvinism into Scotland, France and the southern Netherlands in the late 1550s. For various reasons Calvinists were more militant than Lutherans in propagating and defending their faith with the result that civil disturbances developed whenever their Catholic rulers implemented policies of persecution. Since oppressed Calvinists turned to fellow Protestants in Germany and England for material support, while Catholic rulers tried to maintain a common front against heresy, a confessional polarisation began to form within Europe. As a result, Elizabeth's policy-advisers started to worry that religion would unite the Catholic monarchies of France and Spain against Protestant England, and that they could no longer count on Habsburg–Valois rivalry to protect them from a crusade of European powers. The reconvening of the papal Council of Trent in 1562 encouraged their sense of vulnerability. At Trent, the Roman Catholic Church discovered a new confidence, unity and determination to destroy heresy. It was, therefore, easy for Elizabeth's ministers to believe that the pope would take the lead in binding the Catholic rulers in a league against England (Lock 1996).

The spread of Calvinism led to serious political upheavals in both France and the Netherlands, a situation which had a profound influence on Elizabeth's relations with Philip II and the kings of France. Undoubtedly Elizabeth would have preferred to remain detached from both these conflicts, but neutrality proved impossible as religious and security concerns drew her in.

In the period from 1562 until 1598, France experienced some eight civil wars. Although the wars were partly the product of a power struggle between noble factions during a period of royal weakness, they also had an important religious dimension. Leaders of two of the most powerful noble families (Gaspard de Coligny and the princes of Condé and Navarre) had converted to Calvinism in the late 1550s, whereas their rival (the Guises) had remained staunchly Catholic and opposed any religious toleration. Whichever noble faction managed to win the struggle for power, therefore, would determine the fate of Protestantism in France. The problem for Elizabeth lay in the repeated threat that the Guises would seize power and direct royal policy. Because of their determined stand

9

against the Huguenots*, their international connections and their close ties to the papacy, the Guises were viewed in England as dangerous agents of the Counter-Reformation who were intent on exterminating 'entirely the Protestant religion' (*CSPF 1562*: 4, 39, 47, 55, 70). But the Guise family also posed a more personal threat to Elizabeth. The duke of Guise and the cardinals of Guise and Lorraine were the uncles of Mary Queen of Scots, the Catholic pretender who claimed Elizabeth's throne by virtue of her descent from Margaret Tudor, the elder sister of Henry VIII (see Chart 1). Thus, there was great pressure on Elizabeth to intervene in France whenever it looked likely that the Guises might control the French government.

In the Netherlands, political and religious grievances also combined to create conditions for civil unrest. In the early 1560s, the regent, Margaret of Parma, had difficulty in arresting the growth of Calvinism and blamed English merchants for encouraging and protecting heresy. In 1565 and 1566 the nobility of the different provinces demanded from Philip II and his regent the abolition of the Inquisition* and a relaxation of the laws against heresy. Not all the petitioners were by any means Protestant, but they all viewed Philip's new measures against Protestantism as an attempt to extend Spanish control over ecclesiastical affairs and therefore as part of a drive to undermine their traditional privileges. At the same time, Calvinist preachers were addressing large crowds at open-air meetings in towns throughout the Netherlands, and in the summer of 1566 they led riots in which Catholic religious objects were vandalised and churches desecrated. Outraged and alarmed, Philip II sent the duke of Alva at the head of an army to Brussels to impose military rule and act as governor-general. He arrived in August 1567 and soon afterwards set up a special judicial court known as the 'Council of Troubles' to punish the offenders. The tribunal found guilty nearly 9,000 prisoners accused of rebellion or heresy and put to death over 1,000. Alva's regime alienated Catholics and Protestants alike. His military rule was felt to be oppressive not only in its treatment of dissidents but also in its centralisation policies and imposition of new taxes without consent. Alva was initially successful in suppressing opposition but an armed revolt began in the northern provinces in 1572 and spread to the south during the middle years of the decade. Fighting continued throughout Elizabeth's reign and beyond, and resulted in the formation of the United Provinces (present-day Holland).

The revolt of the Netherlands posed important problems for England. In the first place, Philip's attempts at suppressing the unrest in his territories stirred up fears about Spanish intentions. Elizabeth accepted that Philip's reprisals against his disobedient subjects were entirely legitimate; but, at the same time, she and her councillors were deeply suspicious about the king's motives in sending so large an army to the Netherlands. They surmised that he aimed to employ it against the French Huguenots★ and Protestant England once Calvinism had been eradicated from his own territories. There seemed to be good reason for their mistrust. After all, Alva did not confine his army to its base in the Netherlands. Spanish troops chased rebel leaders into Protestant German areas, and some cavalry went to help the French king against the Huguenots in 1567 and 1569. Furthermore, geography made England particularly vulnerable to an attack from the Netherlands; the deep-water ports and the prevailing winds of Holland and Zealand made the two Dutch provinces an excellent springboard for an invasion of south-eastern England.

Anglo-Burgundian commerce also suffered as a result of the revolt and the Spanish efforts to suppress it. Although the summer riots of 1566 had little adverse effect on the woollen cloth trade, members of the English business community anticipated further unrest, which would disrupt the traffic of goods. Sir Thomas Gresham, the government's financial agent in Antwerp, was so apprehensive about the political and economic future that he advised Cecil 'to consider some other realme and place' for selling English goods (Doran 1999: 107). Initially, the restoration of Spanish authority failed to improve the situation, since it was accompanied by a flight from Antwerp of native businessmen and artisans fearing prosecution. The English community of merchants in Antwerp, moreover, viewed Alva as hostile to their interests, and believed that he intended 'some great mischief' towards them (Ramsey 1986: 56). In particular the Merchant Adventurers★ feared that they would lose their preferential tax rates and be compelled to compete on equal terms with other foreign merchants. As a result of this uncertainty, the secretary of the Adventurers Company went to Hamburg to assess its potential as a destination for English exports, and in March 1567 a three-man delegation set off for the city to negotiate the establishment of a staple there. Although the merchants' unease was completely unfounded, their anxieties were reported in all seriousness back to the English court and intensified the government's own distrust of Alva. Earlier concerns that England was too dependent on the

11

Antwerp mart now looked justified, and questions began to be raised about the value of the Burgundian commercial alliance, even before an embargo introduced in early 1569 suspended trade for four years.

As a result of all these new circumstances, the Elizabethan regime was forced to question traditional assumptions about foreign policy. How important was it to retain the Burgundian alliance? Was military intervention on the Continent possible or advisable? Could Catholic princes be trusted as allies, or should England rely on weaker Protestant groups as confederates in a league? Elizabeth and her ministers also had to respond to a series of international crises, which were unexpected, unfamiliar and fraught with danger. There were no obvious remedies or quick-fix solutions to the various emergencies that blew up in Scotland, France or the Netherlands. Foreign relations under Elizabeth from the late 1560s onwards, therefore, were uncharted waters, which had to be navigated without a compass. The destination that the queen hoped to reach was no different from that desired by all sixteenth-century monarchs: to secure England's defence, to promote its commercial interests, to preserve her own reputation, and to protect the true faith. The route to be taken, however, was by no means clear but rather a matter for debate.

3

TRADITIONAL DIRECTIONS IN FOREIGN POLICY 1558–68

The Habsburg Alliance

Historians disagree about whether or not it was possible for England's 'ancient amity' with the House of Burgundy* to survive Elizabeth's accession and the establishment of a Protestant Church in April 1559. Some historians believe that its days were numbered, particularly given English Protestant hostility towards the Spanish king (Thorp 1984). Philip II was unfairly blamed for the burnings of Protestants in England during his wife's reign, and was known to be an arch-enemy of heresy in his own kingdoms. Therefore, there seemed good reason to expect him to lead or support a Catholic crusade against England. Suspicion on this count appeared to be confirmed when it was learned in England that Philip and Henry II of France had signed a joint commitment to extirpate Protestantism as part of the Treaty of Cateau-Cambrésis (1559). Although Elizabeth was included in the peace treaty, some English observers were convinced that the Catholic rulers were planning 'a united front to exterminate all nations differing from them in religion' (Alford 1998: 53–5). Philip II's marriage the same year to Henry II's daughter also set off alarm bells. It was thought to be another ominous sign that Spanish promises of collaboration with France against international Protestantism had to be taken seriously. Three years later, fears of an international Catholic plot surfaced again when Alva held a meeting with Charles IX of France and his mother Catherine de Medici at Bayonne. Given this climate of fear about an international Catholic league, it is easy to see why some historians believe an end to the Habsburg alliance was pretty much inevitable.

On the other hand, as other historians have pointed out, an important group of people in England (including Elizabeth and Cecil) were keen to retain the traditional Tudor–Habsburg alliance. These figures certainly did not trust Philip and were frequently alarmed by rumours of Spanish hostility towards Protestant England. None the less, they recognised the need to keep the Spanish king and the Austrian Habsburg emperor as allies against the king of France, who seemed the more dangerous enemy at the beginning of the reign. In addition, together with the influential Merchant Adventurers*, they were concerned to avoid any disruption to the traffic in cloth between England and Antwerp, which would almost certainly follow any political rupture (Ramsey 1975).

For these reasons, Elizabeth was careful to nurture her personal relationship with Philip II during the early years of the reign. She treated his ambassadors in an openly cordial way, and took care to explain her policies to them in terms that would reassure the king of her good intentions. Although she dismissed Philip's own proposal of marriage in 1559, she made clear that she was not rejecting his friendship. In 1559 she allowed the Spanish ambassador to think she favoured a marriage with Archduke Charles, the third son of Emperor Ferdinand (see Chart 3). In 1564 matrimonial negotiations were formally re-opened with the Austrian Habsburgs and they continued until the end of 1567, when it was evident that no agreement could be reached over the thorny problem of what religion the archduke would follow while living in England (Doran 1996a).

Historians of England have always argued that Philip II was anxious to continue the close Tudor–Habsburg alliance. Professor Geoffrey Parker's extensive work in the Spanish archives, however, has revealed a more complex picture: at the beginning of the reign Philip II would have liked to intervene in English affairs but found himself without the means to do so. In the early months of 1559, the king's letters expressed his deep frustration at his inability to stop by force 'the evil that is taking place' in England. By the summer, he was tempted to invade the realm and was only restrained by an empty treasury and the call of urgent problems in Spain (Parker 1998: 158). Thereafter, for the next ten years, the problem of England was eclipsed by the danger from the Turks in the Mediter-

14

ranean. During this time, he listened to advisers (including the duke of Alva) who emphasised the commercial, strategic and political advantages of placating and protecting Elizabeth. It was they who pointed out the value of the Anglo-Burgundian commercial connection and the importance of England's strategic position north of the Channel, which made its ruler an essential ally in order to secure the passage of Spanish shipping to the Netherlands (Ramsey 1986). They also argued that it was in the Habsburg interest to have England ruled by a heretical queen (at least in the short term) rather than by Mary Stewart; after all the Scottish queen was not only tied to France by blood and marriage but also prepared to tolerate the Protestant Church in her realm (Doran 1996b). Taking their advice, Philip refused to recognise the claims of Mary to the English throne or agree to papal moves to depose Elizabeth. Even when Elizabeth gave armed aid to the Protestants in Scotland (1560) and France (1563), he did not alter his policy. He was certainly disturbed by her military intervention, and not entirely convinced by her public self-justification that she was acting only to preserve her security and not to advance the Protestant cause. Yet, he remained neutral, and in 1560 even agreed to assist Elizabeth if the French attacked her realm, because of 'the importance to us, and the danger to our dominions if she and her kingdom were lost' (Parker 1998: 152–3). As long as Elizabeth did not openly pose as the defender of European Protestantism and did not help his own heretical subjects in the Netherlands, Philip would not assist the Catholic cause in England by inciting rebellion, agreeing to a papal bull of excommunication, or supporting the pretensions of Mary Queen of Scots.

Thanks to their joint readiness to continue the amity, Anglo-Habsburg relations withstood the mutual suspicions about religion that threatened to destroy it during the first ten years of Elizabeth's reign. The only serious breach before December 1568 arose out of quarrels over commerce and was quickly mended without too much damage to the political amity. This dispute occurred when Philip's regent in the Netherlands unexpectedly placed a temporary embargo on English trade in 1563. Her motives were mixed. She was angry that English merchants were protecting heretics in the Netherlands and irritated by English acts of piracy in the Channel. Most important of all, she was concerned about the impact of the new Book of Rates (introduced by Mary I in May 1558), which had hiked up the duty on English cloth by some 500 per cent, thereby causing a steep rise in its price for Flemish manufacturers. Since the English government offered her no remedies to these and other matters, she decided to extract concessions by prohibiting English traders from entering her ports in November 1563. Her claim that the ban was introduced for the purpose of preventing contagion from the plague then sweeping across England fooled nobody, since the epidemic was already past its peak. Nor did the stratagem work. English merchants, reached an agreement to send their cloth to Emden in East Friesland, which was just outside Spanish jurisdiction. Antwerp, therefore, suffered more than England from the suspension of trade, and Margaret was forced into unconditionally lifting the embargo on 1 January 1565 (Ramsey 1986). This episode, though temporarily disruptive, did no major damage to Anglo–Burgundian relations. As Philip II refused to extend the embargo to Spain, it also had no detrimental impact on Anglo-Spanish relations. In the words of Wallace MacCaffrey: 'There were no complicating ideological considerations; it was a straightforward wrestling match of a kind which had recurred in Anglo-Flemish affairs' (MacCaffrey 1993: 156)

Scotland

Friendship with Spain was so necessary to Elizabeth because of continuing Anglo-French hostility during the early years of the reign. Although the peace of Cateau-Cambrésis ended England's war against France, Elizabeth and her advisers were deeply worried that Henry II would challenge Elizabeth's right to the English throne and seek to supplant her with his new daughter-in-law, Mary Queen of Scots. Early indications suggested to English observers that the French were bent on pushing for Mary's claim to be queen instead of Elizabeth. Henry II refused to restore Calais to Elizabeth at Cateau-Cambrésis on the grounds that she did not have a title to England let alone the French possession. Furthermore, soon after Elizabeth's accession, Mary came to adopt the English royal style in her title and bear the arms of England in her heraldic quartering. In fact, Henry II did not mean to pursue Mary's claim immediately, but just wanted to keep it as a possible lever to use against Elizabeth in the future.

Henry II's death in July 1559 did not remove the threat from France. On the contrary, it was intensified, as his successor was Francis II, Mary's new husband, whose principal advisers were her uncles, Francis Duke of Guise and his brother Charles Cardinal of Lorraine (see Chart 1). Soon afterwards, reports reached England that the Guises were planning an invasion of England for both family and religious reasons. In 1559 it seemed likely that a French invasion would come through Scotland. The 'Auld Alliance' had long posed a danger for English monarchs, but in 1559 French control of Scotland seemed complete: Mary had handed over the crown matrimonial to her husband, thereby reducing her realm to little more than a province of France; a French garrison was based at Leith on the Firth of Forth; and the French-born Mary of Guise was acting as regent. Thus, the 'old postern gate where the Scots could create a diversion had become the front door through which a French army might march' (Dawson 1989: 200–1). It was principally these considerations that led Elizabeth to assist the Scottish Protestant Lords of the Congregation in 1560.

In 1557 the Scottish Protestant nobility signed a document of confederacy called the 'First Band' of the 'Lords of the Congregation', promising to maintain their religion and drive out the Catholics. Over the next year or so, the Lords enjoyed a measure of religious toleration, but the situation became destabilised when Mary Queen of Scots married the dauphin★ and Elizabeth acceded to the English throne. In May 1559, the Calvinist John Knox delivered an inflammatory sermon in Perth, which incited a Protestant riot, and it was soon followed by similar commotions in other towns. The Lords of the Congregation then took up arms in defence of their religion and against French domination. In June they briefly occupied Edinburgh and in October deposed the regent. Naturally, they turned to Elizabeth, their co-religionist neighbour, for help but initially she only lent them money and refused to give military assistance. There were several reasons for her negative response. First, she had serious misgivings about supporting rebels against their legal sovereign. Second, she was anxious to avoid another war against France. Third she heartily disliked Knox, who had launched an attack on female rule in his ill-timed 1558 tract, *The First Blast of the Trumpet against the Monstrous Regiment of Women*, a work which had in fact been targeted at the Catholic rulers, Mary Tudor and Mary of Guise.

In late December 1559, however, Elizabeth was forced to rethink her policy. French troops had arrived in Scotland during August and September, and helped drive the Lords from Edinburgh. Further French reinforcements were daily expected and the Protestant position looked extremely vulnerable. The Lords had also found a persuasive and determined spokesman in Cecil who had recently become converted to a policy of military intervention in Scotland on their behalf. Cecil had supported the Protestant rebellion in Scotland from its inception, even to the extent of tentatively proposing the deposition of Mary Queen of Scots as a first stage in the creation of a Protestant Anglo-Scottish union. During the summer of 1559, however, he had questioned the wisdom of sending English troops to Scotland, preferring to give the Protestant Lords diplomatic and financial aid. By December he had changed his mind and become convinced that only English troops could save the Scottish Protestant cause and defend England from a French invasion coming from the north (Alford 1998).

During the debate on the issue of military intervention, which was held in December 1559, the privy council was divided. Although all the councillors were alarmed by the French threat to England's security, about one-third of them warned against sending an army into Scotland. In the event, Cecil won the day, and the council then united behind a policy of war. They recommended to the queen that a small force of about 4,500 men be mustered and sent north. Elizabeth, however, was not convinced by the arguments in support of a land campaign. She was prepared to send her navy to blockade the Firth of Forth so that French reinforcements could not land at the port of Leith, since she believed that Francis II was intending to build up a stronger military presence in Scotland as a preliminary to an invasion of England. On the other hand, she rejected the council's call for military action on the ground. It was only when Cecil threatened his resignation that she reluctantly ordered an army to the Scottish border under the command of the duke of Norfolk. Even so, she remained cautious and ordered Norfolk to wait in Berwick to see if the Scottish Lords could expel the French without any help from his troops. Among other concerns, she feared that aggressive action in support of the Protestants might alienate Philip II and lead him to retaliate. Within a short while, however, she accepted that the Scottish Lords were powerless on their own. She therefore ratified the Treaty of Berwick (27 February 1560), which agreed to joint military action against the French and future co-operation for mutual defence. In late March, she sent Lord Grey across the border to join the Scottish assault on the French garrison at Leith, but, ever prudent, she began negotiations with Mary of Guise at the same time.

The military expedition was not a success. Grey's assault on Leith was repulsed on 8 May. None the less, after some hard-bargaining, the French capitulated and signed the Treaty of Edinburgh (6 July 1560) which met Elizabeth's war aims. The terms included the withdrawal of all foreign troops from Scotland and Mary ceasing to use the title and arms of England. The French negotiators had been left with few other options: French reinforcements had been prevented by storms from relieving the garrison at Leith; the Scottish regent had died in June; and civil unrest had erupted in France, deflecting attention there away from Scotland. Although Mary Queen of Scots refused to ratify the treaty, Cecil's policy of intervention in Scotland was a notable success. The realm was henceforth governed by a council dominated by the anglophile* Lords of the Congregation. Furthermore, in the summer of 1560, the Scottish council summoned a Reformation parliament, which broke all ties with Rome and established a Protestant Church. England could now enjoy ties of religion and friendship with its northern neighbour.

In many respects, Elizabeth's intervention in Scotland was following the traditional pattern of English foreign policy. Like both Henry VIII and Somerset, the queen had recognised the danger arising from the 'Auld Alliance' and used military force to protect her realm from possible invasion. Following their example, she also developed links with a group of anglophile lords who might use their influence in the English interest. Like Somerset she drew on their shared ideology and common interest in expelling the Catholic French. Yet, there were some differences in her approach. Unlike her predecessors, she treated the Scots as equals and did not publicly assert ancient claims of English sovereignty over Scotland. Nor did she aspire to military control over Scotland and she withdrew English troops from the area as soon as the Treaty of Edinburgh was signed. In addition, she had no thoughts of arranging a dynastic union of the two crowns. She would neither consider the deposition of Mary nor her own marriage to the earl of Arran, whose father was next in line for the Scottish throne. Cecil advised Elizabeth that the Protestantism of the Scottish Lords provided the opportunity for collaboration in the interests of both realms; subjugation of the northern realm was therefore no longer deemed necessary for England's security.

The success achieved at Edinburgh was eroded after Mary returned to Scotland in late August 1561, eight months after the death of her husband. Even before that time, she had refused to ratify the treaty, thereby effectively denying Elizabeth's legitimacy and title to the English throne. But the refusal seemed far more dangerous once Mary was acting as an independent ruler, and English fears about security were thus renewed. In reality, though, Mary's ambitions were focused on the succession, and several times

19

over the next few years she offered to drop her claim to the English throne during Elizabeth's lifetime in return for official recognition of her status as heir presumptive*. Elizabeth, however, rejected this deal. The prospect of a Catholic succession was likely to encourage English papists to rebel or Catholic rulers to invade in order to put Mary on the throne. Besides, many of Elizabeth's Protestant subjects were appalled at the prospect of a future Catholic monarch, and it was unlikely that they would agree to a parliamentary statute legitimising Mary's right to the succession. This disagreement over the succession issue poisoned relations between the two monarchs after 1561 and put a strain on England's ties of friendship with the Protestant lords, who had been transmuted into loyal servants of their ruler on her return to Scotland. English suspicions of Mary intensified in 1565, when she married her cousin, Henry Stewart Lord Darnley, who had his own claim to the English throne (see Chart 1). Elizabeth was so angered by Mary's independent action that for a short while she considered supporting a rebellion of the earl of Moray. The Anglo-Scottish collaboration, constructed so carefully by Cecil in 1560, was therefore in tatters five years later, and England was once again at loggerheads with the monarch of the northern realm (Dawson 1986).

None the less, Elizabeth was furious to learn of Mary's deposition in 1567. In the summer of that year Mary lost control of Scotland after a rebellion of her lords, and was formally deposed in favour of her baby son, James VI. In May 1568 she fled across the border, and was detained in Carlisle before being moved to Bolton Castle. At a superficial level, Mary's downfall seemed a heaven-sent opportunity for Elizabeth; her main rival was now in English hands while anglophile* Protestant lords held power in Scotland. The way looked clear for a return to the amity and league of 1560. But, in truth, Mary's detention in England created further difficulties for Elizabeth. The presence of a Catholic heir presumptive* in England acted as a focus for Catholic conspiracy at home, as when Norfolk made secret plans to marry Mary in 1569. It also opened up a new set of international problems, since Catholics abroad cast themselves in the role of the Scottish queen's protector. As Sir Henry Norris accurately predicted in August 1568: 'there is neither safety to the Queen or quiet to England during the Queen of Scots' abode there...' (*CSPF 1566–8*: 533). Elizabeth, moreover, hated to be a party to a fellow monarch's deposition and exile, since it set a disturbing precedent. She, therefore, offended the new Scottish regent, the earl of Moray, by her anger at his successful rebellion and by her attempts over the next few years to restore Mary by negotiation. Consequently, Mary's flight from Scotland did not result in any immediate improvement in Anglo-Scottish relations.

France

Anglo-French relations also plotted a fairly traditional course during the first decade of Elizabeth's reign. Competing claims to territory in France and security fears about the 'Auld Alliance' continued to be the dominant considerations influencing policy. They both largely explain England's intervention in the first of the French civil wars, although the issue of religion was also a consideration for most of those who supported active aid for the Huguenots★.

The first French civil war (1562–63) was both political and religious in origin. After the death of Francis II in 1560, Catherine de Medici ruled France as regent for her ten-year-old son, Charles IX. Despite her efforts to secure domestic peace, she was unable to contain the political rivalry between the Guises and the princes of Condé and Navarre, the leaders of the Huguenots. Nor could she heal the religious hatred between the Catholic majority and Calvinist minority. In March 1562 the duke of Guise participated in the massacre of a Calvinist congregation at Vassy, which led to Huguenot insurrections throughout the urban centres of France. In April, the Huguenots requested assistance from England but both Elizabeth and Cecil feared the consequences of military involvement, and offered instead to mediate between the two sides and seek a peace to stop 'these extremities' (Doran 1999: 99). In June, fighting broke out across France and rumours reached England that the French Catholics could rely on troops from Spain and Germany. The survival of the Huguenots, therefore, looked to be in jeopardy. For this reason, Elizabeth and her advisers were more receptive when in July 1562 Condé again asked for aid. This time, his agents received a favourable response from the queen. In September, Elizabeth sent an envoy to France to protest at the persecution of 'those who profess the same cause' and to announce her intention 'to act for their preservation' (*CSPF 1562*: 296). The same month she signed the Treaty of Hampton Court, in which she promised to send money and men to France.

Elizabeth and her advisers had different objectives in mind when deciding to support the Huguenots. Cecil was certainly concerned about safeguarding the Protestant cause in Europe. His gloomy prediction was that a Guise victory could well result in the downfall of European Protestantism. Viewing the forces of the Counter-Reformation in a way that had later echoes in the American vision of the Communist threat during the period of the Cold War, Cecil compared the Guise attack on the Huguenots in 1562 to the start of a rock fall which, if left unchecked, would gather momentum and destroy all in its path. But Cecil's mind was also exercised by thoughts of the danger to England's security if the Huguenots were badly defeated. He was alarmed that an overwhelming Guise victory in the civil war would result in an international design 'to promote there nece the Quene of Scotts to the crown of England' (Doran 1996b: 109). Although he had originally balked at sending English troops to France and proposed instead to volunteer loans, by August 1562 inaction seemed to him more dangerous than military involvement (Alford 1998). Elizabeth shared many of Cecil's anxieties about security and religion. Unlike him, however, she also saw in the civil war an opportunity for recovering Calais. She had at first resisted the pale's cession during the peace talks at Cateau-Cambrésis, but had been forced to accept its effective absorption into France. The following year, she had hoped to re-open discussions about its future during the negotiations leading to the Treaty of Edinburgh, but her instructions to Cecil had arrived too late, much to his relief. France's internal divisions in 1562 offered another chance for its restitution. Like her ancestors, Elizabeth recognised that English military success in France was only possible with powerful allies. Henry V had used dissident French nobles to good effect during the Hundred Years' War, and her father had relied on the rebellion of the duke of Bourbon to distract Francis I during his 1523 invasion of France (though in his case far less successfully). Attracted by the prize of Calais, Elizabeth swallowed her dislike of rebels and agreed to send a military force to help the prince of Condé for the sake of dynastic gain. Lord Robert Dudley, her favourite, encouraged her to reach this decision. Although his motives can only be guessed at, his promotion of military adventure certainly opened up the prospect of self-aggrandisement. He may have initially hoped to win military glory by leading an army to France, but it was his brother, the earl of Warwick, who was given command of the English troops. None the less, his advocacy of an interventionist foreign policy in France brought him the political rewards he craved. It enabled him to make the running against Cecil, who had been hanging back from a forward policy, and propelled him into the forefront of policy making. Before May 1562 he had been excluded from the inner circle of advisers; thereafter his counsel was sought over policy towards France, and in November 1562 he was appointed to the privy council (MacCaffrey 1997).

By the Treaty of Hampton Court, Elizabeth sent to France 3,000 soldiers to be used to help Condé and another 3,000 to garrison Le Havre (which the English called Newhaven) and Dieppe. Both towns were to be exchanged for Calais at the end of the war. In October 1562, therefore, English troops entered Le Havre but the war aims of the army were unclear, reflecting the different objectives of the main policy makers. Warwick had no instructions, for example, to aid the Huguenots who were on the defensive in other towns held in Normandy. The main army, therefore, sat kicking its heels in Le Havre while Rouen fell to the duke of Guise's army at the end of November, and Dieppe succumbed soon afterwards. Their capture left Warwick's troops holed up in Le Havre with a hinterland in enemy hands. In December 1562, Condé was defeated and captured, and Elizabeth's policy collapsed about her ears. She was left with the option of either financing the remaining Huguenot forces or withdrawing from France as gracefully as possible. She did neither: she refused to pour good money after bad, which was fair enough, but at the same time she remained determined to hold onto Le Havre and exchange it for Calais in a negotiated peace with Catherine de Medici. Even after Condé reached terms with Catherine (March 1563) and demanded the English evacuation of Le Havre, Elizabeth obstinately made plans for the town's defence and unrealistically continued to demand Calais. The queen's customary caution and pragmatism had deserted her. It was not until May that she began a diplomatic retreat, but by then it was too late. French troops surrounded Le Havre on the landward side, and plague infiltrated the port at the beginning of June. By the end of the month 500 men were dying in a week, and at the end of July the wounded Warwick had no choice but to surrender (MacCaffrey 1997).

Elizabeth's military intervention in France proved an expensive and humiliating failure. It resulted in the loss of 1,500 men and cost some £250,000. In consequence, it marked the last time that English monarchs resorted to arms for the purpose of recovering the lost French territories. Elizabeth refused to admit that Calais was lost forever, but she took diplomatic opportunities to ask for the town's return and did not contemplate using force when her requests were rejected. In the words of Wallace B. MacCaffrey: 'The retreat from Newhaven laid the last ghostly presence of the Hundred Years War' (MacCaffrey 1997: 21). At the same time, the fiasco haunted

Elizabeth and taught her important lessons: foreign allies could not be trusted; continental warfare was highly expensive; and England's military power was extremely limited. These lessons were to keep her out of later French civil wars and the revolt of the Netherlands during the 1570s for as long as she possibly could. She only agreed to send troops to the Continent again when she had run out of other options.

4

CRISIS MANAGEMENT
1568–85

Elizabeth formulated her policies in response to particular crises, and tended to be reactive rather than pro-active in decision making, 'improvising as the situation demanded' (MacCaffrey 1981: 193). She had little other choice. Between 1568 and 1585 the turn of events in France and the Netherlands was unstable and appeared as bewildering to contemporary observers as it now does to history students. Political alignments in France were kaleidoscopic, changing their pattern with every shake-up of power in the civil wars. The political fortunes of the Huguenots* ebbed and flowed over the period, while the policy of the French royal family towards them swung from one extreme to another. Between 1570 and 1572 the Huguenots appeared to have won a secure place in France after fighting three civil wars to gain guarantees of toleration, yet on St Bartholomew's Day 1572 the royal family engineered the massacre of Huguenot leaders in Paris and other cities. In 1573 Charles IX made peace and granted limited toleration to his Huguenot subjects, but his death in May 1574 left them again exposed to the dangers of persecution when Henry III, deemed a fanatical Catholic, took the throne. To the amazement and disbelief of many observers, Henry III then granted religious toleration to the Huguenots, who by 1576 had virtually formed 'a state within a state' in the south. The king, however, faced so many challenges to his authority from all sides that he only managed to keep domestic peace with extreme difficulty. In 1584, civil war again threatened when the death of the heir presumptive* Francis Duke of Anjou left the Huguenot leader, Henry of Navarre, set to inherit the throne on Henry III's death (see Chart 2).

The political configurations in the Netherlands were perhaps less confusing, but the fortunes of the Calvinist rebels there fluctuated so dramatically from one year to the next that it was difficult to make predictions about the future. Thus, the rising against Philip II which had begun in 1566 seemed to have fizzled out completely in 1571. Yet the following year the Sea Beggars* breathed new life into the rebellion when they captured towns in Holland and Zealand. Between 1573 and 1574, the rebels with William of Orange as their leader held out against the Spanish army, but they looked the far weaker side. The spread of the revolt in 1575, after mutinies in the Spanish army, to the whole Netherlands was therefore as unexpected as it was to be temporary. By 1579, provinces in the south had willingly returned to Spanish rule while the north seemed on the brink of military defeat (Parker 1977).

In the British Isles too Elizabeth had to adapt to changing political circumstances. Regent Moray was assassinated in January 1570 and Scotland was plunged into civil war as the supporters of Mary took up arms against the party of James VI. For a time it appeared that the largely Catholic and pro-French Marians would triumph over their Protestant and anglophile* adversaries, a victory which would obviously be against England's interests. The Marians' hostility towards Elizabeth was only too apparent when they harboured fugitives from the rebellion which had taken place in the north of England during late 1569. The Marians also carried out raids over the borders and called upon Charles IX to give them aid. Once more the danger existed that Scotland would become a French base and threaten England's security. With the king's party begging her for aid, Elizabeth had to decide whether or not to intervene in Scotland again. In the event, she provided it with limited financial and military assistance, and with her help the Marians were finally defeated in 1573. The Protestant earl of Morton was then able to rule as a strong regent until his fall from power in 1579 and arrest in 1580, when the thirteen-year-old James VI entered the political stage for the first time. The king's frequent preference for Catholic favourites and his demands to be recognised as Elizabeth's successor introduced a new unpredictability into Anglo-Scottish relations, which lasted until the end of the century.

In Ireland, English control was always precarious, but the Elizabethan regime reeled from one crisis to the next. In 1569 Sir

Edmund Butler, a member of the generally pro-English House of Ormond, raised an abortive rebellion against the English attempts to establish a colony in Munster. The following year James Fitzmaurice Fitzgerald led a rising on behalf of the Catholic cause, which was also defeated. In exile in Spain until 1575, Fitzmaurice arrived in the west of Ireland at the head of a small papal-sponsored force in July 1579, and triggered off rebellions led by the earl of Desmond and Viscount Baltinglass. These insurrections were ruthlessly suppressed, but all pinned down English troops, provided opportunities for foreign intervention, and sent the London government into spells of panic (Palmer 1994). When England eventually went to war against Spain it was Ireland rather than Scotland that appeared the more important security threat to England.

1568–73

Despite English fears about Philip II, there was no steady or inevitable slide into military conflict with Spain. None the less, between 1569 and 1573, there developed a serious breach between the two powers which was never fully repaired. This first major crisis in Anglo–Spanish relations arose over a relatively trivial matter – the affair of the Spanish treasure ships – which spiralled out of control through the shortcomings of the new Spanish ambassador, De Spes. In November 1568 five Spanish ships, carrying bullion to pay Alva's troops in the Netherlands, took shelter in English ports from bad weather and Calvinist privateers★ in the Channel. Cecil immediately raised questions about the legal ownership of the treasure, which the Spaniards had borrowed from Genoese bankers. When the government ordered the bullion to be unloaded as a precaution against theft, De Spes convinced himself that the queen meant to seize the treasure in order to prevent it reaching Alva. He may well have been right. It seems safe to presume that Cecil was intending to arrange for Elizabeth to take over the loan herself, although there is no direct evidence for this interpretation. But, whatever Cecil's intentions, De Spes reacted prematurely when he urged Alva in December to confiscate English ships and property in the Netherlands as a reprisal. Alva's action left no room for negotiation and forced Elizabeth to retaliate in kind. In January 1569 all trade was suspended between England and the countries ruled by the Spanish king, and the lucrative commerce between London and Antwerp was brought to a halt (Ramsey 1986).

Meanwhile, another commercial development was also disrupting Anglo-Spanish political relations. Before Elizabeth's reign, English merchants had made few attempts to diversify into trade beyond Europe and consequently rarely came into conflict with Spain or Portugal who claimed monopolies of trade with the New World. Some London merchants had opened up traffic with Guinea in West Africa in the 1550s, but the government of Mary I had banned commercial activities there in response to protests from Philip II. Elizabeth, however, felt under no obligation to consider the king's interests. She did not recognise the papal treaties, which had partitioned the New World between Spain and Portugal, and she supported the right of her subjects to trade anywhere they chose. Together with her courtiers she invested in several of the more adventurous commercial ventures. As a result of this governmental backing, traders were encouraged to build on the earlier contacts with Guinea and break into transatlantic trade. Thus, in the 1560s John Hawkins embarked on three slave-trading expeditions, which challenged the Iberian★ monopoly in West Africa and the Indies. His aggressive commercial activities, however, affronted the Spanish authorities, while Elizabeth's refusal to prohibit his expeditions aroused intense irritation in Spain. When on the third expedition the Spanish viceroy attacked Hawkins' fleet in the Mexican port of San Juan de Ulúa in September 1568, it was the English turn to feel aggrieved. News of the incident reached England in December 1568, just after the Spanish treasure ships had sailed into the ports of southern England. Whether or not knowledge of the San Juan incident encouraged Cecil to think in terms of retaliation is debatable. What is certain, though, is that the attack on Hawkins together with the Spanish embargo encouraged further English interloping in the Indies and privateering★ against Spain. Francis Drake, a survivor of San Juan, viewed his raids on the Panama area in 1571 and 1572–3 as legitimate acts of revenge for the unprovoked aggression against Hawkins. He and the other sea captains who enthusiastically accepted commissions from the leaders of the Sea Beggars★ and Huguenots★ to attack Spanish vessels were motivated not only by a lust for loot but also by a hatred of a common enemy. After the imposition of the commercial embargo in early 1569, privateering also became an instrument of royal policy. Until 1573 Elizabeth allowed her seamen to prey on the subjects of Philip II, and her ports to be used as bases for French, Dutch and English privateers, thereby further souring Anglo-Spanish relations.

Both Alva's hasty measures against English merchants in December 1568 and the incident at San Juan de Ulúa nourished the burgeoning anti-Spanish sentiment at court. For many Englishmen it confirmed suspicions that Spanish intentions towards Elizabeth were malign. In truth, neither Philip II nor Alva had wanted to provoke a quarrel. None the less, the breach in relations changed Philip's attitude towards Elizabeth and her realm. For the first time in ten years he began to consider ways to restore Catholicism to England by force. In late 1569, he informed Alva that he favoured sending money to the rebels of the North, encouraging the Irish Catholics to rebel and actively supporting Mary Stewart. In 1570, moreover, he welcomed the Anglo-Irish Catholic soldier, Thomas Stukeley, at his court and approved an international conspiracy to assassinate Elizabeth and put Mary on the English throne. The plot was dreamed up by a Florentine banker, Roberto Ridolfi, and involved Mary, the pope, disaffected Catholic nobility in England, as well as De Spes (Parker 1998). That Philip's plans came to nothing in 1569 and 1570 owed much to the unwillingness of Alva to implement them. News of them, however, leaked out to England and Elizabeth started to believe that the Spanish king meant her harm. She, therefore, began to make political overtures towards first the German Protestant princes and then the king of France.

On several occasions during the 1560s, Cecil had recommended that Elizabeth investigate the possibilities of political co-operation with the German Lutheran princes to combat the Catholic threat. Before 1569, however, Elizabeth had no wish to make a formal alliance with the princes for fear that it would put at risk her friendship with the Habsburgs. After the rift with Spain, her attitude changed. An alliance with Protestant Germany looked more attractive on both defensive and commercial grounds. It would provide England with a powerful ally, bring protection for the newly established staple at Hamburg in North Germany, and assist in the development of trade with the Baltic ports. With these considerations in mind, Elizabeth sent an envoy to the empire to propose a formal alliance with the German princes and the Scandinavian kingdoms. The proposal was rejected. The Lutheran princes questioned the queen's motives in seeking an alliance, justifiably believing that she was only interested in obtaining support against Spain. They also had their doubts about her religion, suspecting that she was sympathetic to Calvinism rather than following the Lutheran confession of faith. Most of the princes, moreover, opposed a policy of confrontation with the Catholic powers and preferred to continue in their conciliatory policy towards the Austrian Habsburgs (Kouri 1981).

After the failure of the German negotiations, Elizabeth felt compelled to look elsewhere for a protective alliance. Over the next couple of years, she became uncomfortably aware of her diplomatic isolation and increasingly alarmed at the fresh revelations of Spanish hostility towards her. In October 1570, the Spanish authorities openly welcomed the leaders of the Northern Rebellion to Antwerp. The following year, Burghley uncovered the Ridolfi Plot. Many in England also believed (though in this case erroneously) that Philip II had encouraged and approved the papal bull of excommunication which had been issued in April 1570. With hindsight, it is easy to see that the danger from the Catholic powers was less immediately menacing than most Elizabethans feared. Philip II was distracted by the Turkish threat in the Mediterranean (1570–71) and lacked the financial resources to attack England. The pope could do little harm to England without Spanish support.

Because of the ostensible dangers from Spain and the rebuff from the German Protestants, Elizabeth turned towards England's traditional enemy, France, for an alliance. In late 1570 the time was opportune for opening negotiations. Charles IX had just signed a peace treaty with the Huguenots, some of whose leaders were keen to arrange a marriage between Elizabeth and the king's brother, Henry Duke of Anjou (later to be Henry III). Their objective was to cement the religious pacification in France and to construct a league against Spain in the Netherlands. Charles IX and his mother were also keen on the match and extended a formal proposal in early 1571. Elizabeth and her councillors showed interest and allowed matrimonial negotiations to proceed. The queen, however, did not seek a dynastic alliance as a precursor to a joint Anglo-French venture against Spain in the Netherlands; nor did she want to effect a diplomatic revolution which would mark an end to the traditional Anglo-Habsburg accord. On the contrary, she and Cecil (promoted to the title Lord Burghley in 1571) hoped that an Anglo-French matrimonial alliance would force Philip II to restore commercial relations and 'more curteously use the Queene and her subjectes' (Doran 1996a: 103). They were also looking to cut off French support for Mary Stewart. Charles IX, who had for some time been petitioning for Mary's release from captivity in England and restoration to the Scottish throne, threatened in mid 1570 to send military aid to her supporters in Scotland. The Guises also continued to plan their kinswoman's escape, either by landing troops in

England or Scotland, or by masterminding a Catholic rebellion. A French military presence in Scotland again looked imminent, but this time Elizabeth was to try a new approach. She held back from giving direct aid to the Protestant king's party, and looked instead to arrange a dynastic alliance with the French crown and thereby to nip French intervention in the bud.

The matrimonial negotiations ran into difficulties in the late summer of 1571, when disagreements over religion could not be resolved. They were torpedoed in early 1572 by Henry of Anjou, who had no wish to marry a woman eighteen years his senior and a heretic to boot. His insistence that he should be allowed to attend a full public mass while living in England brought the project to a swift conclusion (Doran 1996a). The Anglo-French discussions, however, did have a positive result – the Treaty of Blois. In the short term its conclusion was a diplomatic coup. Signed in April 1572, it effectively left Mary Stewart out in the cold, and gave Elizabeth a free hand to furnish the party of James VI with military assistance against the Marians. The treaty also ended England's diplomatic isolation, as it provided for the mutual defence of both realms. At the same time, it left the way open for a renewal of Anglo-Spanish relations. As Sir Thomas Smith, the ambassador to France, commented to Elizabeth: if Spain wanted friendship with England, 'nothing is done on your Majestie's part to break the amity' (Doran 1996a: 128). He was certainly right in that the treaty contained no offensive clauses. With the agreement of Burghley, Elizabeth had pointedly refused to follow the advice of Sir Francis Walsingham (her previous ambassador in France) and form an offensive league with France and the German Protestants against Alva in the Netherlands. On the contrary, shortly before the treaty was signed, she and Burghley indicated their readiness to end the rupture with Spain. At about the same time Elizabeth made another conciliatory move towards Philip by taking action to stop the privateering of the Sea Beggars★ and ordering them to leave English ports in early 1572. After the Beggars inadvertently seized the port of Brill on 1 April 1572, she made clear her opposition to French plans for sending troops to fight with them in the Netherlands against Spain. In the summer, she allowed a small force of volunteers under three English captains to occupy Flushing (see Map 1) in order to prevent the port falling under the control of the French.

Barely four months after the Treaty of Blois was signed, Charles IX ordered the massacre of Huguenots, and the Anglo-French treaty seemed hardly worth the paper on which it was written. The St

Bartholomew's Day Massacre was a traumatic event for European Protestants not only because of the scale of the slaughter (some 3,000 died in Paris alone, possibly 10,000 in other parts of France), but also because of its context. In murdering the guests attending the wedding of his sister to Henry of Navarre (the Huguenot leader) the French king had behaved dishonourably, offending ancient rules of hospitality. For Walsingham, who was in Paris at the time of the massacre, no further evidence was needed that Catholics could never be trusted. Many of Elizabeth's Protestant councillors felt the same, and urged the queen to send troops to assist the Huguenots who were defending the bastion of La Rochelle against the royal army.

Elizabeth was equally horrified by the massacre, but she reacted with circumspection. If it was at all possible, she wanted to prevent the consignment of the Anglo-French treaty to the diplomatic dustbin. Otherwise, the French royal family might be propelled into the arms of Spain and once again show hostility towards England by supporting Mary and sending troops to Scotland. The situation in Scotland was particularly delicate at this juncture. Mary's faction there was still resisting royal authority from their stronghold in Edinburgh Castle, and James VI's party was left leaderless after the death of Regent Mar in October 1572. In Elizabeth's view, moreover, a continuance of the entente with Charles might prove more effective than military aid in helping the Huguenots. The massacre had so weakened the French Protestants that they seemed unlikely to withstand the siege of La Rochelle which had begun in February 1573, even with an English force at their side. On the other hand, diplomatic intervention might persuade Charles to agree to a new peace, which would grant the Huguenots security and a degree of toleration. For these reasons, Elizabeth protested angrily to the French about the massacre, but did not break off diplomatic relations. She agreed to be godmother to Charles IX's infant daughter in February 1573 and listened to French proposals for a marriage project with Charles' youngest brother, Francis Duke of Alençon, although he was nearly twenty years her junior. At the same time, she gave the Huguenots unofficial practical help. She allowed England and the Channel Islands to become a haven for religious refugees and privateers, and made no move to stop English volunteers from going to La Rochelle. She also permitted her ministers to arrange the shipment of money, munitions and provisions to the port, and in early 1573 she warned the French ambassador that, if the siege were not soon lifted, she would be forced to supply its inhabitants with military aid. With the recent fall of Edinburgh Castle to James VI's party in Scotland, Elizabeth felt confident about taking this tougher line with the French king. She also offered to mediate between the king and his subjects. Charles IX did in fact make peace with the Huguenots in July 1573, but his initiative had nothing to do with Elizabeth's diplomatic offensive.

The re-opening of the civil war in France in August 1572 persuaded Elizabeth and Burghley that they needed to re-establish amicable relations with Spain. In March 1573 both sides reached an agreement (the Convention of Nijmegen) to restore diplomatic and commercial relations which became formalised into the Treaty of Bristol in August 1574. The settlement was based on the two principles that all merchants should be compensated for their losses and that neither ruler should give refuge to the other's rebels or protect privateers. The treasure, the source of the original dispute, was returned to the Genoese bankers. The recall of Alva from the Netherlands at the end of 1573 also removed a cause of tension between the two countries.

Despite the improvement in Anglo-Spanish relations, there was no return to the situation that had existed prior to December 1568. In the first place, Antwerp never recovered its position as the dominant mart for English woollen cloth, since the commercial life of the city was severely disrupted by the outbreak of rebellion in Holland and Zealand. After their capture of Brill, the Sea Beggars went on to take other towns in the northern provinces including Flushing at the mouth of the River Scheldt. From this base they attacked all shipping directed at Antwerp (which remained in Spanish hands) including vessels carrying English cloth. Even when William of Orange, the rebel leader, allowed the Merchant Adventurers to send a limited number of ships down to Antwerp, marauders so often seized English goods that the river-route was soon abandoned. Instead merchants tried an alternative overland route but this too proved unsatisfactory. Consequently, many English merchants found Antwerp a less attractive destination than formerly and continued using the base at Hamburg. The devastating sack of Antwerp by mutinying Spanish troops in November 1576 (known as the Spanish Fury) drove away the relatively few English merchants who had remained there. They did not return even after the Spanish army left in 1577, since the whole area was by then virtually a war zone and the new Protestant city council was imposing high taxes on foreign merchants to pay for the city's defence. English merchants officially departed in 1582 but, by that time, their commercial activities had dwindled away to virtually nothing. There can be little doubt that the disturbance to commerce between London and Antwerp in the 1570s helped to impair the political relationship between England and Spain. The government no longer had to refrain from annoying Philip out of fear that he would harm English trade. Furthermore, the Merchant Adventurers stopped acting as a pro-Habsburg lobby on the government; indeed some of them became the most outspoken critics of Spain within England and the keenest patrons of privateering exploits against Spanish shipping (Ramsey 1984).

The political relationship between England and Spain was equally damaged by the 1569 breach. Few Protestants in England could forgive or forget the Spanish conspiracies against Elizabeth that had followed in its wake. Elizabeth herself found it difficult to trust Philip and she began spending heavily on military defence. For his part, Philip II continued to be incensed by English help to the rebels in the Netherlands, and blamed the queen for their continuing resistance. Had the revolt in Holland and Zealand petered out soon after 1572, it is possible that Anglo-Spanish relations might eventually have returned to their old footing, but the Spanish attempts to crush the persistent rebellion imposed an intolerable strain on the traditional amity.

1574–81

Thanks to Elizabeth's pragmatism, the English entente with France survived the crisis of August 1572. It was, however, once more put under severe strain in 1574 with the death of Charles IX and accession of the ultra-Catholic Henry III, who was closely associated with the Guise faction. Fearing Guise control of French policy, Elizabeth secretly planned to join a coalition of Huguenots, anti-Guise Catholic noblemen (including the duke of Alençon) and some German Calvinists who were taking up arms against the new king of France. This risky venture, however, came to nothing when the French nobility reached terms with Henry III in the peace of Monsieur 1576.

At odds with France, Elizabeth tried to avoid another major quarrel with Spain and withdrew her support from English maritime ventures in the Spanish Indies, a frequent source of conflict. Until 1576, she also firmly rejected the appeal of the rebels in Holland and Zealand for military aid. If at all possible, she wanted to avoid a direct military confrontation with Spain. Understandably, she lacked confidence that an English army would prove effective against the veteran Spanish infantry, and doubted the value of Holland and Zealand as allies. In addition, she found their rebellion and offer of sovereignty in 1575 anathema to the principle of divine right monarchy, which she embraced. The piracy of the rebels based at Flushing further alienated her and confirmed her view that these men were dangerous rebels who flagrantly disregarded the law. Many of Elizabeth's councillors, however, were less troubled by these scruples. They reminded the queen that the Protestants in the Netherlands were in danger of their lives and that Spain would attempt an invasion of England as soon as the rebellion was quashed. Grudgingly, Elizabeth accepted their interpretation of events and therefore allowed the rebels to be supplied with covert assistance, which did not in fact go unnoticed by Spain. She turned a blind eye to the recruitment of English soldiers who were ready to fight alongside the rebels, and at the same time she tried to prevent Spain from enlisting English volunteers and buying military supplies in her realm.

Despite her undercover aid, Elizabeth presented herself to Philip II as neutral in the conflict. She tried to assure him that she was standing aloof from the rebels who had 'solicited [her] to take possession of Holland and Zealand' and that 'he never had such a friend as she has been' (*CSPF 1575–77*: 76). In 1575 she sent Sir Henry Cobham to Spain to propose mediation based on a settlement which would restore the provinces' traditional privileges, suspend the Inquisition★, and remove foreign troops from Burgundian★ soil. In the spring of the following year, she sent William Davison to the Spanish government in the Netherlands with instructions to arrange a cease-fire. Essentially, the queen wanted the rebellion to end as soon as possible with a negotiated settlement, preferably an agreement which would allowed liberty of conscience and thereby protect the lives and goods of her co-religionists. She believed that the disappearance of the Spanish army from northern Europe would remove the main source of friction in Anglo-Spanish relations. The conclusion of the revolt, moreover, would eliminate opportunities for the French to exploit Spanish difficulties and extend its own influence in the area. Philip, however, took little note of Elizabeth's initiatives. In his eyes she was no impartial mediator but an active Protestant supporter of heresy and rebellion in his territories. Alva's replacement in the Netherlands, Luis de Requesens, on the other hand, was keen to prevent further English involvement in the revolt and intimated that a compromise might be possible.

A new phase of the revolt opened at the end of 1576, after unpaid Spanish troops mutinied and sacked towns in the Netherlands which had been loyal to Philip II. The most notorious incident was the 'Spanish Fury' of November 1576 when some 8,000 people in Antwerp lost their lives. Even before this massacre, all the provinces of the Netherlands had come out in revolt and representatives had been summoned to a States General. Immediately afterwards (8 November) the States* signed an agreement (known as the Pacification of Ghent) with William of Orange, the leader of the rebels of Holland and Zealand. The terms of the Pacification called for the expulsion of all foreign troops from the Netherlands, the suspension of the heresy laws, and maintenance of the religious *status quo* in all the provinces. Initially, the new Spanish governor-general, Don John, accepted the States' demands, and signed the Perpetual Edict in early 1577, but in July he began to organise a new campaign against the rebels. Orange, meanwhile, remained detached from the Perpetual Edict, as he did not trust Philip II or his ministers either to keep the peace or to allow toleration for Protestants.

These events led Elizabeth to re-think her policy. The rebels now seemed to merit her active and open support, since they no longer appeared in her eyes just a small group of pirates and political troublemakers. She also approved of the Pacification of Ghent, whose terms virtually coincided with those she had herself proposed in 1575, and she wanted the Perpetual Edict to provide the basis of a final settlement. It was vital, therefore, that the States continued to exist as a political entity. Elizabeth consequently offered them loans and military aid 'provided they preserved their obedience to the King of Spain' (*CSPF* 1575–77: 481). In the summer of 1577, when it was apparent that Don John would renege on the agreement, Elizabeth began to plan a general Protestant league to defend the States and she sent Daniel Rogers to Germany to present the proposal to the Palatine (the leading Calvinist state in Germany). In September, she agreed to lend the States £100,000 and provide troops if Don John attacked them. For the first time, the advocates of open intervention began to feel confident that Elizabeth would send troops over to the Netherlands. Leicester, their leader on the council, even began planning the composition of the army he expected to head. It was also in the summer of 1577 that Elizabeth approved and provided Drake's naval voyage to the East Indies with three ships and 160 men. This expedition, which ended in Drake's circumnavigation of the world, was intended as much 'to annoy' Philip in the Indies as to discover new commercial opportunities for

36

her merchants (Andrews 1984: 144). Elizabeth maintained this aggressive stance until the end of the year, when she signed a general treaty of alliance, agreeing to send an expeditionary force and money to the Netherlands.

All changed in early 1578. At the end of January, Don John took to the field and roundly defeated the army of the States at the battle of Gembloux. It suddenly seemed inevitable that Philip II would be able to impose an unconditional military settlement on his rebels. In desperation, Orange offered once again to grant the English queen sovereignty in return for her military assistance. At the same time, Catholic deputies of the States turned for aid to the French king's brother, Francis Duke of Anjou (who had been entitled the duke of Alençon until 1576). These events left Elizabeth in a serious quandary. On the one hand, she was certain that a Spanish victory over the rebels would endanger her realm and that the States had to receive some assistance so that they would not submit to Philip II. On the other hand, dispatching an army to the Netherlands would be extremely perilous, given the States' military weakness and political differences. Nor was she happy to take a backseat and allow Anjou to intervene, for fear that the French would be granted influence or territory as a reward for their aid. The council, moreover, was giving her contradictory advice. Whereas Walsingham and Leicester counselled active military intervention in the Netherlands, others recommended caution, while the earl of Sussex put forward a radical plan of his own: in his view, the queen should revive an earlier project to marry the French duke and negotiate a defensive alliance with his brother, Henry III.

In the light of this new situation, Elizabeth immediately scrapped plans to send English troops to the Netherlands: it seemed just too provocative and dangerous. Instead she arranged and paid for John Casimir, brother to the Calvinist Elector Palatine and administrator of the Rhine, to lead a mercenary army into the Netherlands. His presence, she hoped, would strengthen the forces of the States and prevent them negotiating with Anjou. By this means, moreover, she could avoid direct military confrontation with Spain and continue to use diplomatic pressure to persuade Don John to return to the Perpetual Edict. Her policy, however, proved a total failure. The States were dismayed by her change of heart and opened up negotiations with Anjou. Neither Philip II nor Orange would agree to peace on Elizabeth's terms. As for Casimir, his arrival in Brabant in August 1578 exacerbated the religious disputes between the Calvinists and Catholics. According to Professor Charles Wilson,

Casimir's intervention hastened the split of the States into two rival unions, the southern provinces in the Union of Arras★ and the northern, predominantly Protestant ones in the Union of Utrecht★ (Wilson 1970).

Even before Casimir had set off for the Netherlands, Elizabeth had come to favour the Anjou marriage as a way out of the crisis there. Sussex's arguments in its favour had a certain appeal. First an Anglo-French dynastic alliance might frighten Philip into making peace in the Netherlands. Second, marriage to a queen might satisfy Anjou's restless ambition and stop him intervening in the Netherlands as an independent adventurer (for at this time he did not have the backing of Henry III). Finally a dynastic alliance with France might protect England from invasion or international conspiracies, since Henry III would be unlikely to join with Spain and attempt 'eny thing that may be prejudycyall to her Majestie and her husband his brother' (Doran 1996a: 192). In mid 1578, therefore, Elizabeth broached the question of marriage with the French, and throughout 1579 she devoted considerable diplomatic effort to achieving it. During the course of the negotiations, however, her objectives changed. In the summer of 1578, she was anxious to prevent Anjou from heading an army in the Netherlands; but in 1579 she was ready to subsidise him in a military enterprise there, hopefully backed by the king of France. This shift in thinking reflected the desperate circumstances of the rebels. In February 1579, the Catholic provinces in the Union of Arras agreed to open talks with Alexander Farnese Prince of Parma, who had succeeded Don John on his death in October 1578. A few months later, the Union became formally 'reconciled' to Philip II. It was difficult to see how the remaining provinces could hold out against the Spanish army without substantial foreign aid. The only alternative to an Anjou expedition was the dispatch of an English army, and Elizabeth was not yet prepared to take the risk of open war against Spain. During the negotiations, moreover, she began to develop a personal relationship with Anjou and became convinced that he would follow her directions and wishes (Doran 1996a).

In reality, the Anjou marriage scheme was unlikely to provide any solution to the problem of the Netherlands. Anjou was a totally unsuitable agent for the queen, and her trust in him was entirely misplaced. As was to be evident during his later campaign in Flanders and Brabant, he was a maverick who would always go his own way and work only in his own interest. His troops and finances, moreover, were insufficient for rescuing the rebels from Parma's army, even if deployed effectively (Holt 1986). Nor could Henry III act as a useful partner against Spain, for he had neither the resources nor political will to re-open the Habsburg–Valois Wars and give Anjou substantial aid in a Netherlands campaign.

The Anjou marriage did not take place because of the fervent opposition to it within England on religious grounds. The wave of public agitation against the match took Elizabeth completely by surprise. In the council she could rely on the support of Sussex, Burghley, Lord Hunsdon and Sir Thomas Wilson, but Leicester, Walsingham and Sir Christopher Hatton were deeply opposed to it, and by October 1579 they had won over most of the other councillors. Once Elizabeth realised that the marriage was politically impossible, she found herself without any policy at all. Consequently, she was paralysed into inaction on all fronts until the end of 1580. She did nothing to prevent Parma from regaining control of the provinces of Artois and Hainaut and from capturing important towns. She made no move to hamper Philip II in his annexation of Portugal★, and refused to go ahead with a plan put forward in the summer of 1580 to seize and use the Azores in the Atlantic as a privateering base from which to attack Spanish shipping. She also made no attempt to intervene in Scotland, where James VI had approved the execution of Morton and was fast succumbing to the influence of the young French Catholic, Esmé Stuart Sieur d'Aubigny, who had arrived in Scotland in 1579. D'Aubigny, who was widely and probably accurately believed to be a Guise agent, persuaded James to make him duke of Lennox and worked on the king to revive the 'Auld Alliance' and move against the Protestant Church. Elizabeth's hand in Scotland, however, was stayed by the thought that an English operation against D'Aubigny might well alienate the French and put pay to an alliance.

At last, in the early autumn of 1580, Elizabeth decided on action. She dismissed all thoughts of the marriage, and instead proposed to Henry III an offensive military alliance against Spain. Her sudden decisiveness was a reaction to the ever-growing Spanish threat. In September 1580 Philip II had conquered Portugal, thereby gaining an Atlantic sea-board, a sizeable fleet including ten newly constructed fighting galleons, and a second colonial empire, all of which could provide him with resources for an invasion of England. In the Netherlands, peace-talks between representatives of Spain and the States had broken down at the end of 1579, and it had become obvious that Philip II would never concede any effective checks on his authority or any degree of religious toleration. During 1580

39

Parma was preparing for a conquest of the north, having already re-established Spanish control in the lands east of the Zuider Zee. Once these remaining provinces were subdued, there was nothing to stop Parma from invading England (Parker 1977, 1998). Few doubted in 1580 that Philip would order an enterprise against England once his hands were free of the Netherlands. After all, in that year, 800 Spanish and Italian soldiers arrived in Ireland as reinforcements for a garrison that had been established at Smerwick in 1579 by an army in the service of the pope. The massacre of virtually the whole garrison in November 1580 can only be explained in terms of the extreme anti-Catholic paranoia that afflicted the English government and army command.

As terms for the proposed Anglo-French military alliance, Elizabeth suggested that a French army could take on the Spaniards in Flanders, while she would assist opposition groups in Portugal and order attacks on Spanish shipping. Henry III listened sympathetically to her offer of an offensive alliance against Spain, for he too was alarmed at Philip's sudden growth in power, but he disliked the queen's military plan. In his opinion, it was too late to overturn Philip II's conquest of Portugal and Elizabeth should use her resources to help Anjou in the Netherlands. As this difference in strategy emerged during the negotiations, Henry decided to push for the marriage between Anjou and Elizabeth to be consummated before any alliance was agreed. Once married to Anjou, he believed, Elizabeth could not fail to assist her husband financially or be associated with his war against Spain. Without the marriage, there seemed to him a strong likelihood that the French would be saddled with the total expense and danger of fighting the Spanish army in the Netherlands. An Anglo-French marriage, however, was out of the question because of the continuing political opposition to it within England (Doran 1996a). Yet, without the marriage, Henry III refused to sign a military alliance with Elizabeth. Her evident reluctance to commit England to open war against Spain and refusal to make any precise financial contribution to a French assault in the Netherlands aroused in him too many suspicions that she would be an untrustworthy ally.

Surprisingly, Elizabeth was not too disappointed at the failure of the talks to form an Anglo-French league. During the negotiations, she had begun to see advantages in an alternative policy, that of operating unofficially as Anjou's paymaster in the Netherlands. The provision of secret financial assistance to the duke started to look potentially less expensive and dangerous than joining with Henry III in an open league against Spain (Doran 1996a). In August 1581, on hearing that Henry had refused to provide his brother with funds, she therefore stepped into the breach. In one year alone (between 1581 and 1582), she provided Anjou with loans amounting to £70,000. In February 1582 she sent the duke to the Netherlands as her protégé, accompanied by a delegation of forty or so English nobility and gentlemen (Holt 1986).

1581–85

In the event, Anjou's military involvement in the Netherlands neither helped the rebels nor removed the threat to England's security. The duke returned to France in June 1583, having failed to prevent Parma from capturing a string of strategically important towns in Flanders and Brabant. The following year, Parma was poised to attack Antwerp, and it seemed only a matter of time before his army would conquer the entire Netherlands. With the assassination of the rebel leader, William of Orange, in July 1584, the rebels' plight looked desperate. In consequence, Elizabeth renewed her offers of an English alliance to France to 'impeach' Spanish power. Henry, however, showed no enthusiasm for military action against Spain, and stalled throughout the autumn and winter months of 1584. Apart from his persisting suspicions of Elizabeth, the king had his own domestic difficulties to consider. Anjou died in June 1584, leaving the Huguenot★ leader, Henry of Navarre, as heir presumptive★ to the childless Henry III (see Chart 2). To prevent a Protestant succession, Henry Duke of Guise formed the Catholic League★, a paramilitary organisation, and began to look to Spain for funds. A foreign enterprise was impossible at a time when a renewal of the civil wars looked imminent.

Meanwhile, in October 1584 the English privy council debated policy. Initially its members disagreed over whether Elizabeth should intervene directly and send troops to the Netherlands. The interventionists on the council (including Walsingham, Leicester and Hatton) wanted Elizabeth to take the Netherlands under her protection. Others, though (including probably Burghley), feared that this course would be too risky and drew attention to the 'many difficulties' that would result from military aggression against Spain. Instead, they thought that England should look to its own defences and leave Henry III to follow in his brother's footsteps and take the Netherlands under his protection. Eventually, however, the council recommended intervention, but urged Elizabeth to obtain the help of Henry III, John Casimir and Henry of Navarre (HMC 9 *Sal.* ii: 67–70) Consequently, the following month, Elizabeth sent an ambassador to the States★ to investigate the possibility of an alliance, but it was not until Henry III gave a negative answer to the States in March 1585 that detailed negotiations began.

In the spring of 1585, Elizabeth faced her own worst nightmare. She was preparing for war against the strongest power in Europe with only the weakest of allies at her side. Yet, despite justifiable unease, she went ahead with the policy of military intervention. She and her council agreed that war against Spain was inevitable and it was more sensible to fight at the present time as allies of the States than to face a future Spanish invasion alone, once Parma had defeated the north. Few had any doubts that Philip II intended Elizabeth harm, as his hostility towards her was manifest for all to see. In late 1583, Walsingham's spy network had uncovered the Throckmorton Plot, a conspiracy to overthrow Elizabeth, involving the resident Spanish ambassador (De Mendoza), the duke of Guise, Mary Stewart and dissident English Catholics. The following February, another conspiracy in which Spain was believed to be implicated – the Parry Plot – was revealed. In March 1585, the English government learned of the secret Treaty of Joinville, which Philip had recently signed with the duke of Guise as the leader of the Catholic League★. In the treaty, Philip promised regular financial aid to the League so that it could take up arms to prevent Henry of Navarre's accession. Philip and the League, moreover, pledged themselves to banish Protestantism from France and the Netherlands. English paranoia, however, caused Elizabeth's ministers to believe (mistakenly) that the Franco-Spanish collaboration agreed at Joinville was also aimed directly against England. Similarly, when Philip confiscated English shipping and merchandise in Spain in May 1585, the prevailing view in England was that Philip intended to use the vessels as part of an invasion fleet. For this reason, Elizabeth immediately began warlike moves against Spain. In June she authorised a small naval squadron to attack the Iberian fishing fleet off Newfoundland. The following month she gave Drake permission to purchase stores and press men for his voyage 'into forraine parts' (Parker 1998:175).

In August and September 1585, Elizabeth signed the Treaties of Nonsuch with the States. By their terms she agreed to supply her allies with £126,000 a year until the end of the war, as payment for an English force of 6,400 infantry and 1,000 cavalry. In return, they would deliver to her Brill, Flushing and Rammekins as cautionary★

towns. These ports could act as supply bases for her troops operating in the Netherlands. In addition, their occupation was intended as insurance that the States would not make peace with Philip II without her consent and as a guarantee for the repayment of her expenses at the end of the war. Elizabeth turned down the States' offer of sovereignty, since in her view it would lead to 'long, bloody wars' with Philip, and she would only agree to take the provinces of the north under her protection (*CSPF 1584–5*: 571).

While negotiating the treaty of alliance with the States, Elizabeth put effort into a wider diplomatic drive. In April 1585, she dispatched ambassadors to the king of Denmark and the German Protestant princes with the aim of constructing an international Protestant league to counter the Treaty of Joinville. Her specific requests were for troops to assist Henry of Navarre and money to give to the Protestant archbishop of Cologne, who had been driven by the emperor into exile in 1583. The German Lutheran princes, however, refused to join a league or be associated in any hostile acts against the Catholic powers. Not only did they fear retaliation from the Habsburg emperor if they aided foreign Protestants, but they had their own doctrinal disputes with Calvinists and disliked Navarre. The king of Denmark refused to move without them. Only the unreliable John Casimir of the Palatine offered assistance on behalf of the Protestant cause. To make matters worse, Elizabeth's envoys also failed to persuade the Protestant Hanseatic towns to support her in the impending war against Spain. Over the previous decade English merchants had provoked the commercial enmity of the Hanse★ by opening up marts on the Baltic (Emden in 1579, Middleburg in 1582, Danzig from 1579 to 1581 and Elbing in east Prussia in 1581). Elizabeth, moreover, had removed the privileges of Hanseatic traders operating in London. Unmoved by Elizabeth's appeals to the 'godly cause', the Hanse refused to stop supplying Spain with provisions and tried instead to have English merchants expelled from Germany (Lloyd 1991).

Although Elizabeth failed in her attempt to bring the Continental powers into her war against Spain, she did eventually achieve a more limited success in signing a Protestant league with James VI of Scotland. Elizabeth's relations with James had been very uneasy in the years following the execution of the earl of Morton. First, the king's infatuation with D'Aubigny had alarmed the English court. Then, soon after the royal favourite had been forced to leave Scotland, James came under the influence of the earl of Arran, another Catholic who could not be depended upon to pursue

43

policies in the English interest. To ensure that her postern gate remained closed while her troops were abroad, Elizabeth proposed an offensive league with Scotland in the summer of 1585, but Arran took a tough stance and terms could not be agreed. In October 1585, however, Elizabeth's agent in Scotland helped to topple Arran and bring Protestant anglophile* lords into power. Soon afterwards, in early 1586, the queen re-opened negotiations for a league with James VI, and in the summer they concluded the Treaty of Berwick (Lee 1990). The treaty provided James with an English pension and formed the basis of Anglo-Scottish co-operation which continued (though not without periods of mutual suspicion and ill-feeling) until Elizabeth's death.

5

THE CONTEMPORARY
DEBATE OVER POLICY
1558–85

In foreign affairs decision making was a royal preserve, but Elizabeth consulted her councillors on all matters of importance. Their advice was sought at formal meetings of the privy council, either the regular sessions of her inner council or the less frequent meetings of the wider group, which were usually summoned during particular emergencies. Elizabeth rarely attended or chaired these meetings herself, but learned the nature of their discussions and conclusions through her Secretary of State. In addition, councillors individually plied her with informal letters offering advice, while courtiers, ambassadors and other royal servants wrote directly to her with their views on aspects of foreign relations.

Historians disagree about the extent of political consensus within the council, particularly over matters of foreign policy. Some argue that disunity was rare and any differences of opinion concerned tactics rather than overall strategy or international outlook. Steven Alford, for example, has emphasised the 'unity and cohesion' of the council in his recent study of the first decade of Elizabethan polity (form of government), and asserted that on the rare occasions when the council disagreed about policy, it was a 'split based on interpretation: not on religion'. Thus, when Alford looked at the debates over military intervention in Scotland which took place in late December 1559, he argued that 'the privy council divided itself on the practical issues of intervention' but 'agreed on the grounds for action' (Alford 1998: 66–7). This view, however, is open to challenge and it is my view that differences in outlook did play some part in the policy disagreements of the first decade of the reign. Four of the five councillors who initially opposed or were very 'dowtfull towchyng' intervention in Scotland in late 1559 were conservatives in religion and had previously been members of Mary I's council (the marquis of Winchester, the earl of Arundel, Sir William Petre, and Sir John Mason). On the other hand, Cecil, the most enthusiastic advocate of intervention, was a committed Protestant who had helped Protector Somerset during the late 1540s to formulate and execute a policy of Protestant unionism in Scotland (Adams 1984; Dawson 1989). Later on in the late 1560s, there was also a difference in outlook between the supporters and the opponents of the Habsburg matrimonial negotiations. The match came to be promoted by men like Norfolk who were on the whole more conservative in religion and keen to retain the traditional Burgundian alliance. On the other hand, its critics included Leicester and Sir Francis Knollys who strongly objected to the marriage on the grounds of the archduke's religion and demands to hear the mass when living in England (Doran 1996a).

Like Alford, Simon Adams has also tended to dismiss conciliar divisions as insignificant, although he sees co-operation between councillors as a characteristic of the middle years of the reign rather than the 1560s. After 1570, argued Adams, there existed a greater political and religious homogeneity in the council and a corresponding unity over policy. Indeed in his view, between 1570 and 1585 the 'comparative unanimity of the inner ring of councillors provided for a basic political consensus, and maintenance of a common front against the Queen became a pronounced feature of the Council's advisory function' (Adams 1984: 67, 75). In other words, councillors closely collaborated to persuade or batter Elizabeth into following a line of action that they agreed upon but she disliked. There is certainly a case to be made that this form of conciliar consensus operated after 1570 as far as domestic issues were concerned. Elizabeth's inner council held very similar views about Mary Stewart, the succession and the adoption of punitive policies towards Catholics, which contrasted sharply with those of the queen. On the other hand, a consensus is far less noticeable when we look at the debates over international relations, which took place between the early 1570s and 1585.

This picture of a council united over policy in the middle years of the reign has gained greater credence in recent years owing to fresh research into the ideological outlook of Cecil (Lord Burghley after

1571) and Walsingham, who became Secretary of State in December 1573. Closer examination of their papers together with a re-thinking about the culture of political ideology have led historians to challenge the traditional interpretation of both men, which was essentially moulded by Conyers Read during the first half of this century. According to Read, Walsingham represented the outlook of 'aggressive protestants', who were zealots favouring a religious war against Catholic princes. Walsingham, claimed Read, was 'quite prepared to sacrifice English interests for the sake of what he considered the greater cause', namely 'God's glory'. On the other hand, contended Read, Cecil stood for the *'politique'* viewpoint, which placed national considerations before religious ones. As a result, thought Read, Cecil, unlike Walsingham, was prepared to make alliances with Catholic powers in order to safeguard England's security (Read 1913: 35, 36, 58).

Read's analysis, however, underestimated both the Protestant outlook of Cecil and the secular pragmatism of Walsingham. As Stephen Alford, Mitchell Leiman and Malcolm Thorp have shown, Cecil was deeply committed to a religious ideology, which helped shape his policies. He was no *politique*; on the contrary, he could not separate England's national interests from God's cause or the fate of European Protestantism. Thus, like Walsingham, he saw international relations as a struggle between true religion and the Antichrist and expressed a strong sense of solidarity with England's fellow Protestants abroad. It was this perspective that led both men to believe in the conspiracy theories surrounding a Catholic League and to advocate the formation of a Protestant counter-alliance. At the same time, Walsingham had a keen sense of England's political interests, and could view international relations with a secular eye.

Yet, despite this shared mind-set, Cecil and Walsingham did not always reach the same conclusions about foreign policy. Essentially they disagreed on two important issues. First, until the 1580s Cecil was obsessed with the danger from the Guises and Rome, whereas Walsingham believed that the main danger to England came from Spain. Even during the war with Spain, Cecil could not entirely forget his suspicions of France particularly after Henry of Navarre converted to Catholicism. Second, Cecil was always prepared to make alliances with one or more Catholic powers in order to safeguard England from attack. Walsingham, on the other hand, believed after the Massacre of St Bartholomew that Catholics could not be trusted as allies and, even worse, that divine anger might well be aroused if Protestants were to make agreements with idolatrous nations. Walsingham, therefore, preferred to forge a military alliance with European Protestants and also to put his faith in England's own resources for combating the international threats to security. In contrast to Cecil, he generally favoured sending English armed troops to the Continent on behalf of the Protestant cause. In this policy, he could usually count on the support of Leicester. Cecil, on the other hand, tended to work closely with the earl of Sussex, who shared Cecil's deep suspicions of France and dislike of the prospect of military confrontation with Spain.

Thus, despite the greater homogeneity of the council after 1570, it was rarely unanimous in its advice on key foreign-policy issues. Councillors held conflicting views about whether or not the queen should send troops to aid Protestant rebels against their Catholic rulers, negotiate a marriage alliance with Francis duke of Anjou, and publicly endorse Francis Drake's privateering voyages. On occasion, disagreements between councillors led to ill-feeling and bad temper, particularly over the issue of the Anjou marriage. None the less, it is misleading to call their disputes 'factional'. A factional struggle involved groups of people (rather than individuals) who clashed over policy, and 'its essence was a personal rivalry that over-rode all other considerations' (Adams 1982: 34). Consequently, faction resulted in a general lack of co-operation between personal followings. In the field of Elizabethan policy making, by contrast, the queen's leading councillors usually worked closely together. Sometimes, they reached an agreement over foreign policy; no voice, for example, spoke out against the defensive Treaty of Blois with France in 1572, though admittedly Leicester would have preferred a more aggressive league against Spain in the Netherlands while Burghley would have liked a royal marriage underpinning the treaty. Even when councillors held different opinions, they usually co-operated with each other in the execution of policy, and it was rare to see a major rift in personal relationships emanating from conciliar disputes. Policy disagreements only disturbed political life occasionally. Certainly, there were a number of incidents when rows did spill outside the rational debate of the council chamber, and created resentments, hostility and even the threat of personal violence, all of which could be damaging. On the whole, though, quarrels were contained, and political life was relatively smooth and harmonious, at least on the surface, until the late 1590s, when factional rivalry divided the council and rocked the court.

Disagreements over policy helps to explain why Elizabeth sometimes experienced difficulty in following coherent strategies. If

Elizabeth was the pilot navigating uncharted waters, her councillors were the experienced seamen who kept offering contradictory opinions about the course to plot. This point is frequently forgotten by the many historians and biographers who accuse the queen of being indecisive and vacillating in her foreign policy.

Elizabeth did not only rely on councillors for information and advice about international affairs. She also listened to the opinions of merchants and diplomats who were well acquainted with a particular geographical region. Here too she was often bombarded with conflicting advice. The merchants, especially, were not a monolithic pressure group, putting forward the same viewpoint. Those involved in Iberian or Netherlands trade usually tried to promote amicable relations with Philip II, whereas those investing in slave trading or privateering did not flinch from clashes with Spain. Thus, in the late 1560s, Hawkins sought royal backing to continue his attempts to provide the Caribbean empire with African slaves, much to the irritation of Merchant Adventurers in London who were dependent on the Antwerp trade. Similarly, in 1580, Iberian merchants pressed the government to restore Drake's spoils from his privateering circumnavigation of the world in order to avoid a breach with Spain. The investors and sponsors of his voyage, on the other hand, urged the queen to keep the treasure (Kelsey 1998).

As far as Elizabeth's diplomats were concerned, most tended to speak with one voice in favour of promoting the 'godly cause' abroad. After 1570, most of these men owed their positions to Walsingham or Leicester, whose religious and political outlook they shared. Thus, both councillors furthered the career of Daniel Rogers, a frequent envoy to the Netherlands, Germany and Scandinavia between 1575 and 1588. Rogers was the son of the first Marian martyr and was himself a zealous Protestant, strongly committed to the creation of an international Protestant league against the Habsburg powers (Slavin 1994). 'I cannot express', he wrote in 1576, 'how I have (these two years tried to make the Queen take an interest in the Prince's [of Orange] cause' (Wilson 1970: 33). Similarly, Walsingham was the patron of Sir Thomas Bodley, another Protestant zealot. Bodley, who ended his diplomatic career as the English representative on the Council of State of the United Provinces between 1589 and 1598, had studied during his youth at Calvin's Academy in Geneva, where his father had taken refuge as a Marian exile. Because of their godly backgrounds and sympathies, Elizabeth's envoys and ambassadors were able to build up close relations with Calvinist leaders abroad and tended to promote their interests at the English court. In this way, the Elizabethan diplomatic corps did not comprise detached commentators of the international scene, but on the contrary partisans, whose strong religious and political views influenced their observations and opinions.

6

WAR 1585–1603

England in 1585 was militarily stronger than had been the case for perhaps half a century. Elizabeth and her servants had used the years of peace to build up an effective fleet and improve the quality of her fighting men. From 1573 onwards, the queen belied her parsimonious reputation by spending heavily on naval construction, both increasing the number and improving the design of her ships. Although Philip II possessed the larger navy in the 1580s, Elizabeth had 'the most powerful battle fleet afloat anywhere in the world' (Parker 1996: 273). Beginning with the *Dreadnought*, which was launched in 1573, her ships followed a new design that resulted in a sleeker line and longer gun-deck. The effect was greater speed, better manoeuvrability, and more effective gun-power. England's landed forces were also beginning to be modernised in the 1570s, though they still could not compete with those of Spain. Regular training of able-bodied men began in the counties in 1573; soldiers started to be organised in companies under an improved officer corps and command structure; and the new weaponry of pikes and harquebuses★ were slowly introduced. In addition, a small body of experienced officers and soldiers – men like John Norris who had come out of the wars in Ireland and mercenary armies on the Continent – provided the nucleus of a modest professional army. In 1585, therefore, England could deploy abroad a small, well-equipped army, headed by experienced captains, and also muster some 11,000 trained troops and another armed 62,000 men for home defence.

From the very start Elizabeth's war against Spain was a two-pronged affair: a land war on the Continent and a war at sea. Understandably, Elizabeth had only limited faith in the power of English troops to hold back the Spanish army. She and most of her advisers recognised that the navy could do more damage to Spain by disrupting its treasure routes and destroying its shipping. The silver plundered from Spanish vessels could, moreover, contribute to the costs of the troops stationed in the Netherlands.

No sooner was the draft treaty of Nonsuch agreed with the States* than Elizabeth dispatched John Norris to the Netherlands at the head of a force of around 2,500 men. His specific task was to save Antwerp from falling to Parma, but he arrived ten days after the town's surrender (Nolan 1997). Norris' command was clearly a temporary expedient, since the Dutch required someone of noble rank who was close to the queen to take charge of her army. Leicester was the obvious candidate, as it was no secret that he had been for many years in close contact with the leaders of the rebels and a promoter of their cause on the council. Elizabeth, though, 'was not disposed' to use his service (*CSPF 1585–86*: 8). In September 1585, however, she bowed to the inevitable and appointed him commander; he eventually departed for Flushing in December. As English troops began to move into the Netherlands, Drake set off with royal instructions to attack Spanish shipping in Spain and the Caribbean. At the same time Elizabeth put England on a wartime footing by naming lord lieutenants for most counties with the responsibility for mustering men.

Elizabeth did not intend her military actions against Spain to provoke a full-scale war. On the contrary, her objective was to induce Philip II to re-open negotiations with the States and sign a peace treaty on the basis of the Pacification of Ghent. To assist this process, she opened up at least five simultaneous sets of peace negotiations with Spain between 1585 and 1588. She also refused to augment her troops in the Netherlands, and warned Leicester not to 'hazard a battaile without great advantage' (Hammer 1999: 49). When Leicester on his own initiative assumed the title of governor-general in January 1586, she was furious. She had expressly instructed him to refuse any offers of sovereignty on her behalf, since this was the title used by Philip's military representatives in the Netherlands, and Leicester's adoption of it implied that Elizabeth was indeed the sovereign of the United Provinces. In the event she was forced into a compromise by agreeing that he should hold the title under the authority of the States but not herself.

Leicester's two spells of command in the Netherlands were hardly a great success. According to most historians, he made an incompetent general and administrator (Williams 1995). The battle at Zutphen, in which Sir Philip Sidney was mortally wounded, has been described as 'a badly bungled affair' (Nolan 1997: 99). Furthermore, after an initial period of success when the English army repelled Parma's attack on Grave, Leicester failed to stop a number of important towns, including Sluys the gateway to Flushing, falling to the Spanish army (see Map 1). While he was on leave in England, moreover, Sir William Stanley and Rowland Yorke, two men he had trusted and promoted, defected with their Irish regiment to the Spaniards and handed over to them the town of Deventer and the fort dominating Zutphen. To make matters even worse, Leicester quarrelled with Norris (colonel-general of the foot), Thomas Wilkes (one of his own civilian councillors) and the States. He was also responsible for the mismanagement of the queen's finances, which resulted in men deserting for lack of pay, and the overspending of his own budget (Osterhoff 1988). In December 1587, not a minute too soon, he returned to England to be replaced by Lord Willoughby.

By contrast, Drake's depredations in the Indies and raids on the Spanish coasts were extremely effective. In several joint-stock enterprises (in which private investors as well as the queen provided ships for the voyage) Drake was able to injure Philip II's shipping and expose the vulnerability of his defences. In October 1585 Drake launched raids on villages in Galicia in northern Spain. He then moved on to sack the Canaries and Cape Verde Islands on his way to the Caribbean where he captured Santo Domingo and Cartagena. Although the booty proved disappointing for the private investors, it was estimated by one contemporary that Drake had carried out 300,000 ducats worth of damage across the Spanish coast and 300 million in the Indies. The ease with which he penetrated the Indies sent shock waves through the Spanish world, while the attack on mainland Spain was viewed by most foreign observers as an act of war (Andrews 1984; Parker 1998).

Elizabeth's military operations proved a major irritant to Philip II as well as a serious blow to his reputation. For these reasons, the king decided to embark on a grand enterprise against England. Just two weeks after Drake's forces attacked Galicia, Philip accepted a papal invitation to undertake the conquest of England; news of Drake's West Indies raid strengthened his resolve. Throughout 1586 preparations went ahead to amass men, munitions and ships 'with almost reckless haste' and the Armada was ready to set sail in 1587

(Parker 1977: 218–19; 1998). Drake's raids of 1587, however, put back the invasion for a year. In April his men destroyed some twenty-four Spanish ships and considerable supplies in a raid on Cadiz, which led him to brag that he had 'singed the King of Spain's beard'. After a month spent blockading the coast off Cadiz, Drake made for the Azores where he captured a Spanish carrack with a cargo worth £140,000 and burned two of the islands.

In 1588 Philip II launched his Armada. The aim was for Parma to march quickly to London and install a pro-Spanish government. But, the king also had a fallback position. Were Elizabeth to remain secure on the throne, because her Catholic subjects resisted rather than welcomed the Spaniards, Parma was only to occupy Kent. He could then impose on Elizabeth a treaty guaranteeing religious toleration for English Catholics and the withdrawal of her troops from the Netherlands. Given this contingency planning, the political goals of the Armada were perfectly realistic. Spanish military strategy, on the other hand, was ill conceived. The final invasion plan uneasily combined two separate schemes, one proposed by Parma and the other by the marquis of Santa Cruz. A fleet of 125 vessels was to set out from Spain and arrive at a fixed rendezvous in the Channel. There it would act as a bodyguard protecting Parma's force of 27,000 soldiers, which would be transported in barges from Flanders to Kent. For this plan to work, there had to be complete surprise, good weather, exact timing, and excellent communications between Parma stationed in a Flemish port and the duke of Medina Sidonia, the commander of the Armada fleet. Because so much was left to chance, Parma thought the enterprise too risky but Philip did not listen, for he believed that God would favour his crusade and reward him with victory.

Events proved Parma right. The Armada failed to clear English and Dutch ships from the Channel, and as a result the duke's barges could not leave their ports for fear of attack. When the Armada engaged with the English fleet off Gravelines on 8 August, its formation was broken and the Spanish fleet was driven northwards to escape English firepower (Fernandez-Armesto). None the less, the extent of the English victory should not be exaggerated. Elizabeth's navy had neither stopped the Armada sailing through the Channel nor inflicted particularly heavy damage on the Spanish fleet. English action only sank one ship and badly disabled three others. It was the return journey by way of northern Scotland, the west of Ireland and the Bay of Biscay that defeated the Armada. The storms sent perhaps a third of its ships onto the rocks and caused the death of senior officers and maybe two-thirds of its 30,000 seamen.

The defeat of the Armada did not change the balance of sea power in Europe. Within a decade Philip had rebuilt his fleet and he was able to launch three future armadas against England in 1596, 1597 and 1599, all of which were menacing since Ireland was then in rebellion. Yet, from a political point of view the Spanish Armada can be seen as a turning point in the war against Spain. Elizabeth felt keenly Parma's betrayal in pretending to negotiate a peace settlement at Bourbourg in the spring and summer of 1588 while in reality preparing an invasion force. As a result, she lost any lingering trust in Spain and the honour of the Spanish king. She no longer thought in terms of a quick settlement but was prepared for a long drawn-out fight. She also became more adventurous. Instead of following a purely defensive course, over the next six years she agreed to initiatives designed to destroy the power of Spain on a number of different fronts.

In wartime, as in peacetime, Elizabeth was given different advice about what strategy to follow. On the one hand, 'hawks' on her council and in the military command urged her to build up a Protestant league on the Continent and use the English fleet to take the war into Spain by launching an attack on Portugal and seizing vulnerable parts of the Spanish empire. On the other hand, the 'minimalists' (who included Burghley) advised more limited action: continued aid for the Dutch; moderate assistance for the Huguenots against the Catholic League* and its Spanish ally; and use of the navy to destroy Spanish shipping and defend England from another invasion (MacCaffrey 1992). At times, Elizabeth tried to reconcile both these views, but as the decade wore on, the 'minimalists' more frequently won the argument, since the schemes of the 'hawks' (most notably those of the earl of Essex) tended to be expensive and risky. After 1594, moreover, Elizabeth grew increasingly uncomfortable with all her foreign commitments. In the first place, she felt frustrated with her allies, who seemed far too quick to use her forces for their own ends and too slow in repaying her costs. Second, rebellion had broken out in Ulster in 1593 and was proving difficult to contain and impossible to crush. She, therefore, sought to reduce her support for the Dutch and retire from France, and only approved aggressive naval action when convinced that another armada was on its way. By contrast, the 'hawks' wanted the war to be extended. These men were ambitious for military glory (and in some cases private profit), and their hatred of the 'tyranny' of Spain was so strong that they were determined to continue the armed struggle until its power was destroyed.

The first English campaign undertaken after the defeat of the Armada – the Portugal Expedition of 1589 – was the product of a compromise over strategy between the 'minimalists' and 'hawks'. Together Burghley, Drake and Norris agreed on the need for a major military operation to strike back at Spain while its morale was low. After lengthy deliberations, they settled on a three-stage expedition. Drake and Norris were first to destroy the remnants of the Armada, which had limped back to Spain, so that the warships could not be re-equipped and used in a future invasion. They were then to seize Lisbon by trying to kindle a popular rebellion there against Spain in favour of Dom Antonio (the exiled pretender to the Portuguese throne). Finally, Drake was to set off for the Azores and capture one or two of the islands, which could operate as a base for intercepting American silver and goods destined for Spain. Initially, the plan appeared to have some attractive features. The decision to sink the galleons in northern Spain was both sensible and practicable. The expedition (which would be very expensive) was to be organised as a joint-stock venture, which meant that the major cost would be borne not by the queen or taxpayer but by the many private captains and investors who would join it in the expectation of securing booty. There also seemed a strong likelihood of success, since Drake had built a successful career on attacking Spanish shipping and ports (Wernham 1984). None the less, the multiple objectives in the overall plan was a recipe for confusion, while the particular goal of liberating Portugal was unrealistic. Even before the captains set out, many in England had lost confidence in the venture. Elizabeth rightly suspected that her officers were more interested in attacking Portugal than in destroying the Spanish fleet, and she was therefore reluctant to provide the artillery that would make the capture of Lisbon possible. Burghley complained that the queen's costs were rising daily, and Norris had doubts about the feasibility of sailing to Santander or San Sebastian where the Spanish fleet's repairs were taking place (Nolan 1997).

The Portugal expedition was a disaster. Elizabeth's precise in-structions were ignored and the fleet did not sail to the ports where the Spanish warships were harboured. Instead the main fleet went directly to Corunna. There they wasted weeks, while Norris lay siege to a valueless castle and his men drank themselves sick on looted wine. Alerted, the authorities in Lisbon took action to round up political dissidents and strengthen their defences against the forthcoming English attack. When the army eventually arrived before Lisbon, it was no threat at all. Norris' men had been depleted and were exhausted from marching forty-five miles over difficult terrain from the coastal town of Peniche where they had landed (see Map 2). Without heavy artillery, moreover, they had no possibility of assaulting the well-defended town and were forced to retreat (Nolan 1997). Drake tried to salvage something from the operation and set out for the Azores, but he was thwarted by adverse winds. The expedition did not only fail to meet any of its objectives but it also cost at least 8,000, possibly even 11,000, lives (mainly from disease) as well as a sum of £100,000.

The failure of the Portugal Expedition discredited the strategy of taking the war into Spain and resulted in a more limited use of the navy over the next few years. Until 1594, English naval action was mainly confined to privateering and defending home waters. Royal ships were employed in both these activities, but the bulk of attacks on enemy shipping was carried out by individual captains and financed by private investors. Each year between 1589 and 1591, at least 236 private ships were operating in Spanish waters, Europe or the Indies in search of plunder. After 1591 no fewer than 100 ships set out each year from England for the same purpose (Andrews 1964).

Although Elizabeth felt disinclined after 1589 to continue direct attacks on Spain and its colonies, she was forced to extend the war on the Continent and open up a new front in France. After 1589 it became apparent that the States could manage to hold off Spain without much help from her. During and just after the Enterprise of England, Parma's army lost its momentum in the Netherlands and suffered several setbacks. The States, moreover, found a military general of genius in Count Maurice of Nassau, the son of William of Orange, who in 1590 started an offensive against Spain capturing first Breda and after 1591 territory in the north-east, including Zutphen, Deventer and Nijmegen (see Map 1). This reversal of fortunes allowed Elizabeth to divert some troops from the Netherlands to fight in France where they seemed to be needed more urgently. Only a contingent of about 5,000 men remained under Sir Francis Vere to help Maurice and garrison the cautionary towns★, though the queen continued to supply the States with hefty loans.

Ever since she had learned of the Treaty of Joinville, Elizabeth had been haunted by the spectre of Spanish troops moving into France to help the Catholic League★ fight against Henry of Navarre. Although she had few resources to spare for the Huguenot leader, she lent him £30,000 in 1586 to raise a mercenary army. She also allowed his agents to recruit soldiers and buy arms in London. In the summer and autumn of 1589, however, Henry was in desperate need of money and men, his back against the wall in a League-dominated Normandy. After the assassination of Henry III in August, Henry was technically the king of France, but the League put forward an alternative candidate and a bitter war of succession ensued. In response to Henry's pleas for assistance Elizabeth, in late 1589, paid him a further £20,000 and ordered 4,000 men under Lord Willoughby to Normandy where they were to be at the king's command. During their four-month stint campaigning alongside Henry, 'they provided an augmentation to the royal forces, which on several occasions was crucial' to his success (MacCaffrey 1992: 141). Once Henry's military position had significantly improved, Elizabeth withdrew her troops. The following year, however, when Spanish forces marched into northern France, she grudgingly agreed to send reinforcements again. Fear that Philip would use the Channel ports as a launching pad for an invasion of England or Ireland caused her intervention. In 1591 she ordered two expeditions to France: first, 3,000 men under Norris to Brittany to expel the Spanish garrison established at Blavet on the south-east coast (see Map 3), and later 4,000 men under the earl of Essex to Normandy to co-operate with Henry in the siege of Rouen. Both campaigns went badly. The siege of Rouen got off to a slow start because Henry had other priorities and Essex disregarded Elizabeth's instructions. The siege eventually commenced on the last day of October, three months after Essex had landed in France, by which time the English army was seriously depleted. Very reluctantly, Elizabeth agreed to send reinforcements but their arrival in April 1592 coincided with the retreat of Henry's army (Lloyd 1973). In Brittany Norris and his French allies fared no better. At Craon in May 1592 they suffered a heavy defeat with severe losses. Another 4,000 soldiers were sent to Brittany but to little purpose. Norris participated in some indecisive skirmishing before moving his army into Paimpol in September 1593 (Nolan 1997).

None the less, during 1594 the threat to England from continental Europe began to subside. In the Netherlands, the Dutch successfully captured Groningen, the last major Spanish fortress in the north. In France, Henry won a series of victories after the death of Parma and his conversion to Catholicism in July 1593. At last in February 1594 he was crowned king at Chartres, and the next month he entered Paris. Although his war against Spain continued, the danger from the League was virtually over and the Spanish threat to Normandy had also come to an end. Spanish troops, however, continued to hold important strategic points in Brittany, which caused problems for England. In early 1594, they occupied Crozon (see Map 3) overlooking Brest harbour and began building modern fortifications there in preparation for a siege to take Brest. Military planners in England advised Elizabeth that the sheltered area of Brest harbour would be an ideal spot for the preparation of another armada to invade England, and urged her to employ the navy in a combined land and sea operation to destroy the Spanish fortresses around Brest. Persuaded by their arguments, Elizabeth ordered a naval squadron under Sir Martin Frobisher to be shipped to Brittany in 1594 to join up with Norris still based at Paimpol. In the autumn, the English captured the castle of Morlaix and the Spanish fort at Crozon, but Frobisher was wounded in the fray and died soon afterwards of gangrene poisoning (Nolan 1997).

By the end of 1594, therefore, Elizabeth was in a position to disengage from Continental Europe. She had secured her main objectives: there was now little danger of Spain occupying the Channel ports or overrunning the northern Netherlands. She could therefore concentrate on suppressing rebellion in Ulster. Consequently, no sooner had Crozon fallen than Elizabeth began to recall her troops from France and order them directly to Ireland. At the same time, Norris was transferred to a new command in Ulster. Elizabeth only reversed this policy of Continental disengagement for a short period, just after the Spaniards took Calais in April 1596. On this occasion she dispatched 2,000 troops to Picardy, but immediately withdrew them after the town was recaptured by joint Anglo-French forces the following year. Her decision to extricate herself from France was supported by the 'minimalists', Burghley and Robert Cecil. The earl of Essex and the 'hawks', however, were deeply disappointed that she did not continue to fight against Spain on the Continent.

None the less, over the next three years the hawkish group on the council was successful in winning Elizabeth's approval for three major naval offensives against Spain. Intelligence reports that Philip was preparing a new armada, 'farre greater then in the year 1588', convinced the queen and Robert Cecil that they had to take pre-emptive action to counter the threat from Spain (Hammer 1999: 247). The first of these naval offensives was a plan devised by Drake and Hawkins to raid Spanish shipping and capture Panama, the isthmus through which Peruvian silver had to pass. Panama was, however, too well defended, and the enterprise ended in failure and the death of both generals from sickness (Andrews 1984).

The second naval operation was a strike on the Spanish fleet at Cadiz in 1596. It was a great victory. The English fleet with Dutch help took the Spanish completely by surprise, captured the port, and burned or captured some fifty-seven ships. Yet, despite its success, the expedition exposed some of the recurring problems that haunted the military campaigns against Spain. First, the quest for booty took precedence over the strategic aims of the expedition. As a result, while the soldiers were occupied in sacking Cadiz, they allowed two of Philip's new galleons and twenty-eight merchant ships to be sunk by their crews and escape capture. Second, no sooner did the fleet put out to sea than Elizabeth lost control of the enterprise. Instead of following her instructions, Essex tried to highjack the expedition and activate an ambitious plan of his own for establishing a permanent English garrison in Cadiz. Instead of looting and leaving the port, as the queen had ordered, he attempted (unsuccessfully as it turned out) to bounce her into accepting its use as a base for naval operations against Spanish lines of communication with the Indies and Baltic. Third, as occurred in so many other campaigns, the English commanders fell out. In this case Essex and Lord Admiral Howard quarrelled over Essex's initiative. In the event, Howard refused to leave a garrison in the port without the express authority of the queen and ordered Essex home (Hammer 1999). Finally, the expedition failed in its primary purpose to stop a Spanish invasion attempt. No assault was made on Philip's main fleet harboured at Lisbon. In October 1596 an armada set off from there with the aim of seizing a base in England or Ireland. Luckily for Elizabeth, it was dispersed by a gale off Finisterre.

The following year, a third English naval offensive was launched. This time, Elizabeth agreed to the kind of grand strategy that had been advocated by Essex the previous year. In July 1597 the earl was given command of a naval expedition to attack Spanish shipping at Ferrol and to establish a base on one of the islands of the Azores. But storms, inadequate supplies and sickness among the troops prevented the 'grand strategy' from getting off the ground, and Essex had to abandon both the assault on Ferrol and the occupation of the Azores. His desperate attempt to scrape some victory by capturing booty was also a failure; the English navy missed the Spanish treasure ships, though only by a margin of a few hours (Hammer 1999). Even worse, the absence of the fleet in the Atlantic left English waters undefended, and another Spanish armada (smaller than the Grand

Armada of 1588 but still of sufficient size to cause trouble) was able to sail towards Cornwall before a storm drove it back to Spain. After this debacle Elizabeth was never again tempted into one of Essex's grand designs. Not only were they expensive failures but they took her shipping out of home waters leaving England exposed to invasion. Furthermore, they seemed irrelevant to her needs after 1597. In June 1598 rebellion once again broke out in Ireland under the leadership of Hugh O'Neill, earl of Tyrone. In August, O'Neill won a resounding victory over an English army at Yellow Ford and by the autumn practically all of Ireland was lost to the queen. Ireland, consequently, became the overriding concern for Elizabeth's government.

Ideally Elizabeth would have liked an end to the Anglo-Spanish War. She had explored the possibility of peace in 1595, but Spain had then shown little interest. In May 1598 Philip II signed the peace of Vervins with Henry IV. A few months afterwards in September the Spanish king died, and his successor, Philip III, indicated that he would consider a peace with England. The English council was divided over what policy to follow. Cecil favoured peace, but Essex and the hawks argued that the war had to be pursued until Spain was on its knees, since the word of Catholic rulers could never be trusted.

Elizabeth, herself preferred a policy of peace. In August 1598 she signed a treaty with the United Provinces of the Netherlands which renegotiated their old alliance. By its very nature, she was effectively recognising her ally as an independent state. She also dramatically reduced her financial commitments in the area and arranged for the repayment of English loans. A little later, she agreed to open preliminary peace talks with Spain. But in the informal meetings held between the two sides in 1600, the mutual distrust was so strong that the representatives could not even reach agreement over matters of protocol. There was no way that Spain would agree to her requirement that that the United Provinces should be included in the peace and recognised as virtually independent under the formal sovereignty of Spain. For the rest of the reign, low-level talks continued between London and Brussels but they did not develop into formal peace negotiations.

With the failure of peace talks, Philip III agreed to help O'Neill in the hope that it would drive the queen to make concessions at the negotiating table. In 1600, about 3,400 Spaniards landed at Kinsale in Munster, where they awaited reinforcements from O'Neill. Kinsale was a poorly chosen site. It was hundreds of miles from

O'Neill's base in Ulster, and a large English army led by lord deputy Mountjoy swiftly moved to surround the Spanish garrison there. Mountjoy's troops, however, were forced on the defensive, when the armies of the Irish chieftains marched south to relieve the fortress town and attacked his rear. In the battle that followed the Irish army was routed and nine days later, on 12 January 1602, the Spanish garrison surrendered. Over the next year the O'Neill rebellion was brought to a close, and the chieftain submitted six days after Elizabeth died. Altogether it had cost England nearly £2,000,000, which was more than the total expenses of the war in France and the Netherlands.

7

CONCLUSIONS

Although Elizabeth took counsel over foreign policy, she of course held strong opinions of her own. She had her own brand of prejudices and convictions, which came into play whenever decisions had to be made. Her approach to international affairs has been almost invariably described as cautious and conservative: her commitment to peace and the traditional Habsburg alliance before 1585 being characteristic of her caution; her advocacy of the rights of monarchs and dislike of rebellion as indicative of her conservatism. According to Charles Wilson, Elizabeth's most uncompromising critic, this conservatism was both 'obstinate' and 'obsessive', a form of a social snobbery that helps explain her unwillingness to form any kind of alliance with the mercantile communities of the northern Netherlands (Wilson 1970: 127).

At the same time, many historians have doubted Elizabeth's sympathy for the Protestant cause abroad. Conyers Read and R.B. Wernham set the tone in their various works which highlighted the importance of national security in English policy, and represented the queen as indifferent to religious matters (Read 1925, 1955, 1960. Wernham 1966, 1980). In the words of Read: 'The one thing that mattered to her was the peace and security of England, and she was far from identifying those objectives with the Protestant cause' (Read 1960: 309). More recently, Dr Kouri has also claimed that Elizabeth had little sympathy for the Huguenots and Dutch Protestants 'who were both rebels and inflexible Calvinists', and similarly argued that national interests rather than religion dominated her dealings with foreign powers (Kouri 1987: 426).

Although there is some truth in these views, to my mind they represent an oversimplification of Elizabeth's position. Certainly the queen wanted to avoid war against Spain, but she was no appeaser and on several high-profile occasions was prepared to risk offending Philip II. She did not, for example, abjectly seek to explain De Spes' 'misunderstanding' in 1569 and restore the Genoese treasure immediately to Alva; on the contrary, she risked further alienating Philip II by threatening in 1570 to sell-off the goods she had confiscated from Spanish merchants the previous year. In 1581 she publicly knighted Drake after his piratical circumnavigation of the world, and distributed much of his booty to the investors of his voyage. The following year, she openly sponsored Anjou's military expedition against the Spanish army in the Netherlands, and allowed English nobles and courtiers to attend his coronation as duke of Brabant (a title which was then held by Philip II).

In addition, Elizabeth was far from immune to the plight of her co-religionists abroad. It is undoubtedly true that, unlike Cecil and Walsingham, she did not actively seek to extend Protestantism abroad. Because of her commitment to the principle that the ruler should determine the religion of the state, she was prepared to live in a Europe where two (or even three) Christian faiths co-existed. Consequently, she did not put pressure on Philip II to grant his Protestant subjects freedom of worship in their own churches. On the other hand, she would not sit idly by, passively watching her co-religionists being butchered by their fellow-citizens or oppressed by their rulers. Even before 1585, she repeatedly gave them diplomatic aid and connived so that they received private military and financial support from her subjects. Of course, security issues played a part in her motivation but, judging from her public statements, so did a sense of identity with European Protestantism, for she frequently presented herself abroad as the protector of Protestants though not of rebels (Doran 2000). This distinction was not too difficult to maintain in relation to the Huguenots, as she could with some justice claim that they were taking up arms against the Guises and not the French crown, which had issued edicts of toleration. Similarly, she could just about persuade herself that the Scottish Protestant lords in 1559 were fighting to protect their liberties against the French rather than taking up arms against their legitimate sovereign. Such a position, however, was far more difficult to uphold when it came to the case of the Calvinists in the Netherlands. Here, therefore, she took a different stance. During the first decade of the Netherlands Revolt, Elizabeth tried to distance herself from the rebel leaders who challenged Philip II's rule. At the same time, she openly gave asylum to the tens of thousands of Protestant refugees, who fled the Spanish authorities in fear of their lives, and also petitioned Philip to suspend the Inquisition* so that his subjects could have freedom of conscience. It was only when it became apparent that Philip would not accept any religious compromise and that the Calvinists could survive only with her help that this fiction broke down. Elizabeth then justified her intervention by branding Philip a tyrant and a danger to the whole Protestant world.

It is now fashionable to claim that Elizabeth had no foreign policy and merely reacted to the problems that beset her (Wilson 1970; Ramsey 1984; Nicholls 1999). It is true that there were periods when Elizabeth seemed overwhelmed by the complexities of the international situation and at a loss as how to proceed; plenty of examples can indeed be found when she dithered or prevaricated. None the less, she did pursue consistent general aims and objectives, and in this sense had a foreign policy. Her goals were primarily defensive and, unlike her father and indeed many of her subjects, she entertained no dreams of expansionism in France, the Americas or the Indies; or if she did dream them, 'she permitted them little intrusion upon reality' (Lloyd 1973). Her first priority was security. To defend her borders she was prepared to use force to keep the French out of Scotland and the Spaniards out of Ireland. She also endeavoured through a mixture of diplomacy and military action to eliminate the dynastic challenge that came from Mary Queen of Scots and her foreign allies. To prevent a joint invasion by the Catholic powers, she tried to keep on amicable terms with both France and Spain for as long as humanly possible, and when she quarrelled with one she made political overtures to the other. She also tried to stop either of them building up a fleet or army along the coastline of Northern Europe that could be used in an attack on England. She could usually rely on Spain to keep the French out of Flanders but the presence of the Spanish army in the Netherlands proved more of a problem. At first she believed she could obtain its withdrawal by means of diplomacy, but eventually she was convinced that force was required. A secondary aim, but one that was still important, concerned the defence of European Protestantism; as already demonstrated, wherever possible she tried to save her co-religionists from annihilation. Third, Elizabeth was mindful of England's economic interests. Financially dependent as she was on customs dues and on loans from the City of London, she had to protect and extend English trade by giving diplomatic support to her merchants when they attempted to find new staples, markets and sources of raw materials in Europe and beyond (Doran 1999). It was this commercial consideration that lay behind most of Elizabeth's dealings with Russia and the Baltic cities and states. During the war years it led her into negotiations with the emperor to counter the lobbying of the Hanseatic towns who wanted him to expel her merchants from Germany.

In recent years historians have been divided about the effectiveness of Elizabeth's handling of foreign relations during the years of peace. Some have been highly critical, emphasising her hesitancy and accusing her of doing 'too little too late' to help the Dutch rebels and French Huguenots (Ramsey 1984; Wilson 1970). The most scathing criticism has come from Charles Wilson who argued that the queen missed a vital opportunity to ally with William of Orange in 1576. Her failure to take on the leadership of the revolt at that time when the Netherlands were united against a bankrupt Spain, he claimed, caused an end to the fragile unity among the provinces. As a result, not only did the south return to Spanish rule but Elizabeth ended up having to rescue the northern provinces, when they were on the military defensive from Parma, and thereby condemned England to a long, hard war against Spain.

In my view, however, these criticisms of the queen are mainly unfair. Elizabeth's instinct in resisting calls for direct military intervention in the Netherlands before 1585 was certainly understandable and probably sound. The disunited provinces had a poor record in warfare and were likely to prove an unreliable ally. Direct aid to them would have been seen by Philip as an act of war and might well have resulted in the suspension of Anglo-Iberian★ trade, which was growing ever more profitable. Had intervention taken place in the mid 1570s, it is doubtful that a rapid victory would have followed, for Spain recovered very quickly from the 1575 and 1576 mutinies. Counter-factual history is always problematic, but there is good reason to suppose that earlier intervention would have left Elizabeth more vulnerable to military defeat, as reforms to her navy and army were only just underway. Nor would early intervention necessarily have ensured the union of the whole Netherlands, as Wilson has postulated. It is difficult to see how the provinces could have been kept together, considering the religious, political and social differences that lay behind the split of 1579.

None the less, it cannot be denied that Elizabeth sometimes made mistakes in her handling of foreign relations. In general terms, she was badly informed about affairs in Spain and the Netherlands where after 1566 she relied on spies and agents for information. Spies told their paymasters what they wanted to hear, and consequently filled Walsingham's post-bag with alarmist reports about Catholic conspiracies during the 1570s and early 1580s. Consequently, Elizabeth and her ministers frequently overestimated the danger from international Catholicism. They failed to appreciate, for example, that Alva favoured a conciliatory policy towards England, and their suspicions towards him were usually misplaced. Had Elizabeth appointed resident ambassadors to Spain and the Netherlands, some of these misapprehensions might have been avoided. On particular occasions, moreover, Elizabeth's decisions were not very sensible. The Le Havre expedition, the overreaction to Mary Stewart's deposition, and the support for Drake's 'circumnavigation' (which did a great deal to provoke Philip into sending troops to Ireland in 1580) were particularly questionable and harmful (Parker 1998). Perhaps most bizarre of all was the Anjou marriage scheme. Not only was it unlikely to provide a solution to her international problems, but Elizabeth's concentration on it for three years prevented her from taking swift action on other important fronts.

Despite some errors of judgement, Elizabeth's foreign policy had important successes during the years of peace. English aid to the Scottish lords (1559–60) not only furthered the Reformation in Scotland but also protected the northern border, though here praise is due to Cecil more than Elizabeth. The evacuation of French troops was vital to England's security and Elizabeth also did well to stymie French initiatives to recover influence there again after the 1560s. At the same time, Elizabeth successfully retained the friendship of the Catholic kings of France between 1572 and 1585, which assisted her in her dealings with Spain and Mary Queen of Scots. It is also arguable (though ultimately unprovable) that her diplomatic and financial aid to the Calvinists in France and the Netherlands helped their morale and contributed to their survival. During the years of peace, moreover, she did not neglect to prepare for war, and her financial support allowed the English navy to modernise and grow. Last but not least, she helped her merchants find new marts in Baltic ports when the staple at Antwerp began to founder, and gave them diplomatic assistance in their attempts at diversification into new areas such as Russia, Turkey and Persia.

Elizabeth's record as a war leader has come under even greater fire from hostile historians. In the past, she has been criticised for excessive caution, indecisiveness, parsimony and a failure to control her commanders. Elizabeth was certainly not at her best during the war years. Again and again, she no sooner issued orders for an offensive than she revoked or modified them. She repeatedly released far fewer soldiers for foreign service than her allies demanded or her military advisers recommended. Consequently she was frequently squabbling with Henry IV and the States★ about money, men and strategy. When she did agree to large-scale enterprises, such as the Portugal and Panama expeditions, the stated goals were often too disparate while her instructions to commanders were unclear, or at the very least open to different interpretations.

In the realm of warfare Elizabeth's gender made the conduct of war far more difficult. Unlike her father she could not take control of a campaign from the field of battle. Her military leaders, moreover, had little confidence in a woman's competence to deal with military matters, and they often went their own way and disregarded her instructions. In the pithy words of Christopher Haigh: 'A woman could browbeat politicians and seduce courtiers, but she could not command soldiers' (Haigh 1988: 142). Her age was also a liability. By the 1590s, she had outlived most of her trusted advisers and was forced to rely on younger men whose judgement she often questioned and whose outlook she did not share. Some of them, in their turn, considered the queen well past her prime, and grew frustrated with her risk-aversion policies and disinclined to follow her instructions.

It should not be forgotten, though, that Elizabeth was hamstrung in her war effort by the inadequacies of the military machine at her disposal. In naval campaigns, she was dependent on ships and captains paid for by private investors who were more interested in winning booty than in national security. They deliberately misconstrued her instructions for personal advantage, with the result that the queen had no effective control over expeditions once they were at sea. As for the army, she had no permanent force and had to conscript men who were often reluctant to serve abroad. Levying troops put great strains on the administrative and financial resources of her realm. It is no wonder that she was unwilling to burden the country with the cost of large-scale and lengthy campaigns on the Continent, and thought hard before agreeing to any ambitious military proposal.

Elizabeth did in fact devote large resources to the war effort and was far less penny-pinching than her some of her critics suggested. For her campaigns on the Continent she conscripted about 106,000 men (an estimated 11 per cent of the eligible male population); some 37,000 also served in Ireland. At a time when her annual revenue was around £300,000 a year, the war in Brittany cost her at least £191,878; the expenses incurred in Normandy and Picardy amounted to at least £97,461; and after 1585 her charges in the Netherlands were around £120,000 per annum. It has been estimated that the total cost of eighteen years of warfare reached £4,500,000. This included about £320,000 on the war in Ireland and £1.5 million on the navy (Wernham 1984, 1994; Parker 1996). In paying for the war Elizabeth used up her financial reserves in the Exchequer and spent well beyond her ordinary income. She was therefore forced to resort to expedients that weakened the crown (such as selling crown lands and taking out loans from the City of London) and were unpopular in the country (for example the sale of monopolies and exploitation of purveyance). The burden on the country was immense in other ways too; the counties had to bear the cost of recruiting and training the militia, defence fortifications, and military recruitment. This major war effort was carried out against a backdrop of economic depression, dearth and plague. Not surprisingly, complaints were expressed in the parliaments of 1597–8 and 1601, and disturbances took place in several coastal regions of the south, where the burdens were greatest. Given these conditions, it is a mark of the strength of Elizabethan government that the country did not experience widespread social and political unrest.

Although individual campaigns were rarely spectacular and often unsuccessful, the money and effort were not wasted. It is of course impossible to know how well the Huguenots and Dutch would have fared without English aid. Yet, because her financial and military contributions usually arrived at the lowest points in their fortunes, English intervention may well have been crucial. The arrival of Leicester's troops in Holland initially lifted morale just after the loss of Antwerp when Parma looked set to subjugate the northern provinces. Similarly, Elizabeth's loans and auxiliary troops assisted Henry of Navarre in his darkest hours, enabling him to keep up the fight against the superior forces of Spain and the Catholic League. The huge sums spent on the navy also brought returns. While the weather was certainly crucial in seeing off the Spanish invasion attempts, Elizabeth could usually count on her navy to protect the Channel. In addition, the navy proved its worth in the amphibious operation against Brest harbour in 1594 and in the many raids on Spanish convoys. Her ships made commercial life difficult for Spain and hampered its war effort in France and the Netherlands. Overall therefore, despite the queen's own personal weaknesses and the limitations of her military machine, she made an important contribution to the international war effort against Spain. By her death, moreover, her main objectives were fulfilled: England's borders were secure; the Spanish presence was removed from France; France was kept out of Flanders; the power of Spain was 'impeached' but not destroyed; the United Provinces were free from the threat of Spanish military rule; and Protestantism was tolerated in France and supreme in the United Provinces. Elizabeth's policies were not solely responsible for these outcomes, but they undoubtedly helped. Historians have been so keen to revise the myth of the glorious Elizabethan war against Spain, as promoted in swashbuckling Hollywood films and old-fashioned nationalistic texts, that this achievement is sometimes overlooked.

SELECT BIBLIOGRAPHY

There is no readily accessible collection of documents on Elizabethan foreign policy for use in the classroom. Students and teachers can find a few extracts of value in Susan Doran, *England and Europe 1485–1603* (Harlow, 1996b) and Geoffrey Regan, *Elizabeth I* (Cambridge, 1988). I have made some reference in the text to documents in the *Calendar of State Papers Foreign Elizabeth* at the Public Record Office (*CSPF Eliz.*) and Lord Burghley's collection of papers in the *Calendar of the Historical Manuscripts Commission of Salisbury Papers at Hatfield House* (HMC 9 Sal.). Another invaluable printed calendar is *Calendar of State Papers Spanish*, ed. G.A. Bergenroth, P. de Gayángos and M.A.S. Hume (1862–99). Useful documents on explorations can be found in relevant volumes of the Hakluyt Society, especially the second series volumes 142 (1972), 147 (1976) and 168 (1981). On naval campaigns see also J.S. Corbett, *Papers Relating to the Navy 1585–87* (1898) and R.B. Wernham (ed.), *Expedition of Sir John Norris and Sir Francis Drake to Spain and Portugal 1589*, Navy Records Society, 127 (1988).

For the European background

Mack P. Holt, *The Duke of Anjou and the Politique Struggle during the Wars of Religion* (Cambridge, 1986).
C. Martin and G. Parker, *The Spanish Armada* (London, 1988).
Geoffrey Parker, *The Dutch Revolt* (London, 1977).
—— *The Grand Strategy of Philip II* (London, 1998).

71

There are several useful short surveys of Tudor or Elizabethan foreign policy

Susan Doran, *England and Europe in the Sixteenth Century* (Basingstoke, 1999). Provides an up-to-date thematic survey of the whole century.

Mark Nicholls, *A History of the Modern British Isles 1529–160: The Two Kingdoms* (Oxford, 1999). Particularly useful on Scotland and Ireland.

R.B. Wernham, *The Making of Elizabethan Foreign Policy 1558–1603* (Berkeley, CA, 1980). This is readable and useful but beginning to show its age.

Penry Williams, *The Later Tudors 1485–1603* (Oxford, 1995). This is a more general textbook but contains a fairly detailed narrative of foreign relations.

More detailed discussion can be found in the following

Wallace T. MacCaffrey, *The Shaping of the Elizabethan Regime* (London, 1969).

Wallace T. MacCaffrey, *Queen Elizabeth and the Making of Policy 1572–1588* (New Jersey, 1981).

Wallace T. MacCaffrey, *Elizabeth I: War and Politics 1588–1603* (New Jersey, 1992).

Wallace T. MacCaffrey *Elizabeth I* (London, 1993). Summarises the earlier three studies.

Those with an appetite for narrative will also find the following invaluable

R.B. Wernham, *Before the Armada: The Emergence of the English Nation 1485–1588* (London, 1966).

R.B. Wernham, *After the Armada: Elizabethan England and the Struggle for Western Europe 1588–9* (Oxford, 1984).

R.B. Wernham, *The Return of the Armadas: The Last Years of the Elizabethan War against Spain 1595–1603* (Oxford, 1994).

The following *biographies* provide dense narrative as well as *an interpretation of Cecil and Walsingham* now under attack

Conyers Read, 'Walsingham and Burghley in Queen Elizabeth's privy council', *English Historical Review* 30 (1913), pp.34–58. A useful summary of his views on the two men.

Conyers Read, *Mr Secretary Walsingham and the Policy of Queen Elizabeth*, 3 vols (Oxford, 1925).
Conyers Read, *Mr Secretary Cecil and Queen Elizabeth* (London, 1955).
Conyers Read, *Lord Burghley and Queen Elizabeth* (London, 1960).

A revisionist approach to the politics of the court and the foreign policy of William Cecil and Francis Walsingham can be found in the following

Simon Adams, 'Faction, Clientage and Party: English Politics, 1550–1603', *History Today* 32 (1982), pp.33–9.

Stephen Alford, *The Early Elizabethan Polity: William Cecil and the British Succession Crisis* (Cambridge, 1998).

Jane A. Dawson, 'William Cecil and the British Dimension of Early Elizabethan Foreign Policy', *History* 74 (1989), pp.196–216.

Mitchell Leiman, 'Sir Francis Walsingham and the Anjou Marriage Plan 1574–81', University of Cambridge Ph.D. (1989).

Malcolm Thorp, 'William Cecil and the Antichrist: A Study in Anti-Catholic Ideology', in Malcolm R. Thorp and Arthur J. Slavin (eds), *Politics, Religion and Diplomacy in Early Modern Europe. Sixteenth Century Essays and Studies 27* (Kirksville, MI, 1994).

Other works

S. Adams, 'The Protestant Cause: Religious Alliance with the European Calvinist Communities as A Political Issue in England 1585–1630', University of Oxford D.Phil. (1973). This influential thesis has sadly not been published but it has informed all major studies of the war years.

Simon Adams, 'The Queen Embattled' in Simon Adams (ed.) *Queen Elizabeth I: Most Politick Princess* (London, 1984).

—— 'The Lurch into War', *History Today* (May 1988).

K.R. Andrews, *Elizabethan Privateering: English Privateering during the Spanish War 1585–1603* (Cambridge, 1964).

Kenneth R. Andrews, *Trade, Plunder and Settlement: Maritime Enterprise and the Genesis of the British Empire 1480–1630* (Cambridge, 1984).

Gary M. Bell, 'Elizabethan Diplomacy: The Subtle Revolution', in Malcolm R. Thorp and Arthur J. Slavin (eds), *Politics, Religion and Diplomacy in Early Modern Europe* (Kirksville, MI, 1994).

Keith M. Brown, 'The Price of Friendship: The "Well Affected" and English Economic Clientage in Scotland before 1603', in Roger Mason (ed.), *Scotland and England 1286–1815* (Edinburgh, 1987), pp.139–63.

Jane A. Dawson, 'Mary Queen of Scots, Lord Darnley, and Anglo-Scottish Relations in 1565', *The International History Review* 8 (1986), pp.4–24.

Susan Doran, *Monarchy and Matrimony: A Study of Elizabeth I's Courtships*, (London, 1996a). This has much to say about Elizabeth's relations with France, Spain and the Empire before 1585.

Susan Doran, 'Elizabeth I's Religion: the Evidence of her Letters.' *Journal of Ecclesiastical History* (forthcoming in 2000).

Felipe Fernandez-Armesto, *The Spanish Armada: The Experience of War in 1588* (Oxford, 1988).

Christopher Haigh, *Elizabeth I: Profile in Power* (London, 1988, 2nd edn 1998).

Paul E. J. Hammer, *The Polarisation of Elizabethan Politics: The Political Career of Robert Devereux 2nd Earl of Essex* (Cambridge, 1999).

Harry Kelsey, *Sir Francis Drake: The Queen's Pirate* (New Haven, CT, 1998).

E.I. Kouri, *England and the Attempts to Form a Protestant Alliance in the Late 1560s: A Case-study in European Diplomacy* (Helsinki, 1981).

—— 'For True Faith or National Interests? Queen Elizabeth and the Protestant Powers', in E.I. Kouri and Tom Scott (eds), *Politics and Society in Reformation Europe* (Basingstoke, 1987).

Maurice Lee, *Great Britain's Soloman: James VI and I In his Three Kingdoms* (Urbana and Chicago, IL, 1990).

Howell Lloyd, *The Rouen Campaign 1590–92: Politics, Warfare and the Early-Modern State* (Oxford, 1973).

T.H. Lloyd, *England and the German Hanse, 1157–1611: A Study of their Trade and Commercial Diplomacy* (Cambridge, 1991).

Julian Lock, 'How Many Tercios has the Pope? The Spanish War and the Sublimation of Elizabethan Anti-popery', *History* 81 (1996) pp.197–214.

Wallace T. MacCaffrey, 'The Newhaven Expedition, 1562–1563.' *Historical Journal* 40 (1997), pp.1–21.

John S. Nolan, *Sir John Norreys and the Elizabethan World* (Exeter, 1997).

F. Osterhoff, *Leicester and the Netherlands 1586–87* (Utrecht, 1988).

William Palmer, *The Problem of Ireland in Tudor Foreign Policy 1485–1603* (Woodbridge, 1994).

G. Parker, 'The *Dreadnought* Revolution of Tudor England', *Mariner's Mirror* 82 (1996), pp.269–300.

G.D. Ramsey, *The City of London in International Politics at the Accession of Elizabeth Tudor* (Manchester, 1975).

—— 'The Foreign Policy of Elizabeth I', in Christopher Haigh (ed.), *The Reign of Elizabeth I* (Basingstoke, 1984).

—— *The Queen's Merchants and the Revolt of the Netherlands: The End of the Antwerp Mart* (Manchester, 1986).

—— 'The Settlement of the Merchant Adventurers at Stade, 1587–1611' in E.I. Kouri and Tom Scott (eds), *Politics and Society in Reformation Europe* (Basingstoke, 1989).

M. J. Rodriguez-Salgado and Simon Adams (eds), *England, Spain and the Gran Armada 1585–1604* (Edinburgh, 1991).

John J. Silke, *Kinsale* (Liverpool, 1970).

N. Sutherland, 'The Foreign Policy of Queen Elizabeth, the Sea Beggars and the Capture of Brill, 1572', in *Princes, Politics and Religion, 1547–1589* (London, 1984).

Malcolm R. Thorp, 'Catholic Conspiracy in Early Elizabethan Foreign Policy', *Sixteenth Century Journal* 15 (1984) pp.431–48.

Charles Wilson, *Queen Elizabeth and the Revolt of the Netherlands* (London, 1970). A highly critical account.